Butoh Dance Training

of related interest

Anna Halprin
Dance – Process – Form
Gabriele Wittmann, Ursula Schorn and Ronit Land
Forewords by Anna Halprin and Rudolf zur Lippe
ISBN 978 1 84905 472 0
eISBN 978 0 85700 851 0

The Moving Researcher
Laban/Bartenieff Movement Analysis in Performing
Arts Education and Creative Arts Therapies
Ciane Fernandes
ISBN 978 1 84905 587 1
eISBN 978 1 78450 034 4

Mudras of Indian Dance
52 Hand Gestures for Artistic Expression
Revital Carroll with Cain Carroll
Cards Set
ISBN 978 1 84819 175 4
eISBN 978 0 85701 142 8

Butoh Dance Training

Secrets of Japanese Dance through the Alishina Method

Juju Alishina

Translated by Corinna Torregiani

SINGING
DRAGON
LONDON AND PHILADELPHIA

Disclaimer: Readers should consult a qualified medical practitioner before adopting any exercises in this book. Neither the author nor the publisher takes responsibility for any consequences of any decision made as a result of the information contained in this book.

First published in 2015
by Singing Dragon
an imprint of Jessica Kingsley Publishers
73 Collier Street
London N1 9BE, UK
and
400 Market Street, Suite 400
Philadelphia, PA 19106, USA

www.singingdragon.com

Front cover image © Francis Lepage
Copyright © Juju Alishina 2015

Library of Congress Cataloging in Publication Data
A CIP catalog record for this book is available from the Library of Congress

British Library Cataloguing in Publication Data
A CIP catalogue record for this book is available from the British Library

ISBN 978 1 84819 276 8
eISBN 978 0 85701 226 5

Printed and bound in Great Britain

CONTENTS

Part 3 Application

Preface

My teaching experience in this field

This book is the English version of one published in Japan in January 2010. In 2013, the French version appeared in France.

I am thus all the more delighted that this book is being published in English and will be distributed in English-speaking countries. The Japanese and French versions caught the interest of both professional and amateur dancers and received good press coverage.

This is a method which is constantly evolving within my teaching practice. Each year I enrich it with new exercises. In 2009, I decided to publish my book in Japan when my career was reaching a turning point and I wanted to refer to all my years of research.

Being ephemeral, dance is not easy to convey. I would like this book to produce similar effects to a cookbook. Just like gourmets who are willing to travel great distances to taste dishes crafted by a particular chef, some students—from other European countries, the United States, Brazil or Asia—travel to Paris to attend my classes. Recipes allow chefs to create new dishes for their restaurants and allow readers to be initiated into cooking at home with their family. The same can be said of my method: through this book you will be able to train in this practice even if you are on the other side of the world.

My teaching technique is primarily geared towards European, American and other foreign students. I introduce Japanese traditions and ways of using the body starting from the basics, assuming that there is no mutual understanding without prior knowledge.

I convey aspects of Japanese culture even though, over the last 17 years, my life has been influenced by European culture. I married a French man, I gave birth in France and I live in French society. My life is therefore governed by the French ways of doing things.

Through the melding of the Japanese and French cultures, I hope to create more universal and global ideas, an aesthetic and a teaching technique, and go beyond the traditional distinction between East and West.

I have been dancing on stage since I was 19 and I evolved through self-training. This method is the real means through which I experienced my body. My technique will remain even after my departure. Zeami's *Fushikaden* (*Transmission of Style and the Flower*)[1] is still here hundreds of years after his death and it will always exist. I am the only one who can do certain kinds of things which are situated somewhere between the origin of Butoh and the new generation, belonging both to Japan and western countries. After the founding of my dance company in 1990, I always intended to create and develop my own technique to leave it for posterity.

The body expression I have created is considered to be contemporary dance, Butoh and traditional Japanese dance, but at the same time, it is none of these things. It is dance which involves multiple aspects. Since 2001, more than a thousand people have attended my classes and today I have dedicated over a thousand hours to them. I would like to draw greater recognition and awareness to this new body expression and to see it advance academically.

My work involves weaving two threads: the chain links, representing time—and texture, representing space. Time is music and history (past, present, classical and modern). Space is fine arts and geography both in the East and West.

The technique introduced in this book is composed of exercises I created and others derived from traditional Japanese dance and Butoh that I adapted and tailored. When known, I state their origin. All the exercises have been performed in my classes and the results have been proven. I experimented with all of them on myself. Feel free to select the ones you want to practice.

---

1   N.d.T.: Zeami Motokiyo (c 1363–c 1443), also called Kanze Motokiyo, was a Japanese aesthetician, actor and playwright Zeami wrote several treatises on drama, the first of which was the *Fushikaden* ("the transmission of the flower through (a mastery of) the forms," more loosely "style and the flower"), known colloquially as *Kadensho* (*The Book of Transmission of the Flower*). It is the first known treatise on drama in Japan.

This technique originates from the notes and advice I used to leave for my students who replaced me when I was on tour. This is why I sometimes address teachers and sometimes students and participants.

I would like this book to be read not only by students and teachers but also by anyone interested in starting this form of dance or learning about it. The teaching in this work involves all dimensions of human life, and I hope that everyone who reads this may be led to reflect on the different ways of knowing one's own body.

Juju Alishina
Paris, 2015

THE FUTURE OF BUTOH

My dance is composed of two branches. On the one branch, the "traditional dance," which was handed down as a system. On the other, the "avant-garde dance," which is constantly changing and plays a ground-breaking role. First I will talk about Butoh as an avant-garde form of dance and about the relationship I have with this art.

What kind of dance is Butoh? Each type of dance has its own formal and technical features. For instance, one can be initiated into classical ballet, tai-chi-chuan, flamenco or belly dancing by starting with the codes governing the dance, since the music, technique, costumes and accessories are all clearly defined.

Butoh, on the other hand, is more comparable to abstract painting. It has no scenic rules. Butoh dancers are often believed to have shaved heads or very long hair, naked bodies painted white or tattered kimonos. But if these dress codes are not respected, this does not necessarily mean that it is not Butoh.

Technically speaking, Butoh can include choreography which expresses physical disabilities through movements of the knees and hip joints or using *uchimata* movements (pigeon-toed walking), convulsions, disarticulation and other movements addressing one's awareness and weight towards the earth instead of the sky. Some choreography makes manifest not only human beings but all sorts of animals and plants. However, when these techniques are not used, this does not mean that it is not Butoh.

Defining Butoh involves a number of difficulties since its essence relies on one's own perceptions. Butoh performances require imagination and reflection skills to be developed by the dancers as well as the audience. Nonetheless, when I am asked to define Butoh, I say that it is "an avant-garde dance created in Japan in 1959" and I then describe the Japanese social background of that period, since Butoh cannot only be considered a performing art; it is also closely linked to social changes and an evolution in ways of thinking.

Butoh was created and developed as an underground culture during the Japanese economic boom. In the 60s and 70s, Japan witnessed a series of phenomena similar to those taking place in the United States and Europe.

During the 80s, social movements supporting underground cultures began to weaken and communities like Butoh groups dissolved and declined throughout the world.

When I was 20, at the beginning of the 80s, I lived in one of these Butoh communities called *Byakko-sha* in Kyoto. This group lasted longer than others, but in the middle of the 90s and exactly ten years after I left, it dissolved. Each member of this community was called to make his or her own path. Some changed careers, some became freelance and solo dancers, and others created their own companies and continued practicing Butoh. Some dancers who were part of the *Byakko-sha* are still active on the international scene.

The differences between Butoh communities and American dancers, for example, can be found in their principles. American dancers seemed to believe in freedom, equality and democracy, while Japanese communities were based on a rigorous hierarchy. Moreover, even if there is no relationship between Butoh and religion, Butoh has been compared to the innovative religious movements which arose in those years. Nevertheless these communities share similarities, as many of their members are intellectuals who have led an ascetic life detached from this world, searching for different values.

When I created my own company in Tokyo in 1990, hippie culture had nearly disappeared. Society no longer welcomed vagabond, eccentric artists. In the golden age of the "underground," Butoh and life—or fantasy and reality—overlapped. Today the trend is rather to oppose daily life in favour of art, private life to work in all fields. Butoh is now taught in dance schools and cultural centers and is becoming more accessible. This was unthinkable when I was young. In the 70s and 80s, people would say to me: "I'd like to go to Butoh performances but I don't dare, it scares me," or "I know neither where to find Butoh shows nor how to get in." But now that Butoh has become like other performances, one can approach it more easily, see performances and attend classes.

The artist's life has a huge influence on their art. My current works would be different if I didn't live in France. Moreover, my ability to enter into Butoh mode is due to my experiences in training camps when I was young.

Today, some young people do not manage to learn to dance Butoh even after years of training because their environment is completely different from the "underground" that used to be. They can no longer seem to grasp Butoh as an avant-garde dance. Instantly becoming an avenging spirit, a demon, an animal or even smoke in a dance hall or on stage while preserving the same values as a mere mortal, requires much more concentration, mental elasticity and imagination than ordinary life can provide. Studying only in a studio or at a school often produces no more than a useless dance, like flavorless fruit.

Nevertheless, since yoga (which was considered a secret technique) can be practiced even by ordinary people in rented or borrowed spaces in practically any town, in some associations, or in the middle of malls, one should be happy that Butoh practice has become more popular. If one wants to deepen one's learning of yoga, one can potentially take the next step and go to an *ashram* in India, the source of this discipline. Nowadays, although Butoh is more widespread, each individual is responsible for developing their own level of ability. It is not uncommon to see students who began learning in my class in Paris (not in Japan) achieve a respectable level after a number of years.

The globalization of Butoh

France was the first European country which adopted Butoh. Thanks to their success in France, *Sankai Juku*[1] or *Kazuo Ohno* could develop their activities. But Butoh is not the only example. There are a number of historical examples, such as the Russian ballet or Isadora Duncan, that gained acclaim after their stay in France. Historically speaking, France is the center of European culture.

---

1   N.d.T.: *Sankai Juku* is an internationally known Butoh dance troupe. It was founded by Ushio Amagatsu in 1975. Since then, *Sankai Juku* has performed in 44 countries and visited more than 700 cities around the world.

I came to France in 1997, after having been invited by the *Maison des Cultures du Monde* to represent Japan at the *Festival de l'Imaginaire*. Each country (Germany, India, Ethiopia, Turkey, Bangladesh and so forth) was represented by a music or dance group selected for the festival. My company, *Nuba*, had already performed in France at the *Festival d'Avignon* in 1993. However, my stay in 1997 carved out the direction I would take from that moment on.

Today, the underground theater *Bertin Poirée*, located in Châtelet, the heart of Paris, is a Butoh center. Since 1999, every year in June a Butoh festival has taken place, in which I have participated several times. At this occasion, participants from Japan as well as other foreign countries are brought together. In recent years, there has been a great number of people who do not come from Japan, including some of my students. This underground theater welcomes experimental creations. It has become a meeting place both for experienced dancers and beginners who want to train; this is very positive.

In an interview for New Caledonian national television, I was asked why Butoh had been so well-received in Europe. I replied that it has "something universal that touches the soul deeply and meets the needs of Europeans." I answered spontaneously since it was a live broadcast, but later I kept reflecting on this question.

It is widely believed that Japanese culture can be exported abroad only if it is accompanied by a certain air of exoticism. However, by practicing Butoh in Europe, I realized that its main concept could only be welcomed here because of the source of inspiration from Surrealism and Dadaism.

In general, the very exotic is often too difficult to understand. For instance, the *enka*, a traditional Japanese chant dating back to the Showa era, is not popular in Europe. Its words and modulations are too Japanese and too different from European traditions. On the other hand, thanks to its structure recalling the great operas, kabuki is considered representative of Japanese culture and is welcomed by Europeans.

Butoh has been adopted in Europe, but some unfortunate misunderstandings still occur. For example, people tend to believe that Butoh is nothing but the expression of one's emotional side and tend to disregard the technical aspect of the dance. Some theaters refuse to hold Butoh performances claiming that they tarnish the stage, are ugly and evoke dangerous thoughts. However, Butoh varies: its style changes according to the dancers and schools. My hope is that people will grasp the overall essence of Butoh and not only see "the tip of the iceberg."

People attracted to Butoh are those who are aware of the "wild beast hiding within them," see Part 2, 2.6 *The baby, the beast.* However, it is true that it is difficult to tame this "dangerous beast." Consequently, in some scenes dancers seem to move without any limitations or control, projecting their own emotions and personal disorders. To dominate this wild animal inside oneself and find one's way in the arcana of Butoh as a performing art, one should not only refer to the "beast" as the basis for expression, but should also learn the technique and the dramatization. These are also components of the objectives of the Alishina technique.

Photo: Eiichi Miyajima
Dancer: Juju Alishina
1990 Tokyo

The generations of Butoh

Butoh came to light in 1959 on the occasion of the performance of *Kinjiki* (*Forbidden Colors*) by Tatsumi Hijikata. Dancers who started their careers in the 50s and 60s are generally considered to be the first Butoh generation. Those who began in the 70s are the second, those in the 80s, the third, those in the 90s the fourth and finally those in the new millennium, the sixth generation. Butoh thus developed quickly: although in terms of relatives a generation extends over 30 years, Butoh generations span ten years.

Between the third and the fourth generation two important changes occurred: the decline of Butoh communities and Butoh's globalization. Around 1990, after years of Japanese predominance, Butoh granted access to foreign dancers for the first time.

As I started in 1982, I am considered part of the third generation, the one which saw the biggest changes.

As a third-generation dancer, I strongly wish for Butoh—my roots—to continue flourishing while I affirm my own dance technique, which was not limited by the Butoh concept in any way. My dance is not "typical" Butoh. I started training in this style, until I realized that this kind of training didn't suit me, so after extensive trial and error, I modified my approach. My dances and choreography are thus original and represent a singular aspect within the Butoh universe. I studied traditional Butoh technique, but I am not a direct disciple of Tatsumi Hijikata. Accordingly, I do not wish to perpetuate standard Butoh. My desire is to create an original dance, which is something that I consider to be more relevant: a dance which has its own features yet keeps its foundations in Butoh.

Making a "New Butoh" implies both facing scenic issues and the question of the system itself. Since Butoh is not governed by any system such as the *iemoto* and the *natori*[2] in traditional Japanese dance (*Nihon-Buyoh*) and teaching certificates, grades or dans as in judo or kendo do not exist, arguably one becomes a Butoh dancer through "self-assignment." I sometimes have the impression that, especially in Europe, every single amateur could, one fine day, do a Butoh

---

2   These terms refer to the organizational model in traditional Japanese arts.

performance. This freedom and ambiguity in the way Butoh works is positive but also implies some risks.

This simplicity is also accompanied by a lack of productivity. For instance, I was able to give classes and workshops officially only after 12 years of training. Does this not seem like a long detour? This seems especially evident when comparing the years needed to become a professional Butoh dancer with those needed to qualify as a schoolteacher. The latter can teach after a short university course. And then there are modern dancers who become officially qualified soon after having been given their diploma.

The lack of a system in Butoh means that one must be sure of one's own dance quality and one must wait for favorable conditions. This produces a series of inconveniences and a lack of productivity. In creating this technique and a system for Butoh, I would like to allow the next generations of dancers to overcome the ambiguity I faced.

When I am away from Paris, I try to leave my classes to my students as much as I can. If they can train to teach classes properly and in the right environment, they will be able to provide high-quality teaching when they go off on their own. This also gives hope to other students. It is important to have successors.

I would like Butoh to continue growing and developing without losing its primordial essence (like *bujutsu*—a military art—and yoga, which were both created this way).

Some fear that mass production could ensue, but I do not think this should be cause for worry. In my opinion, one should instead think that the more low-quality products there are, the more the price of high-quality products will increase.

There are of course some people who do not consider any Butoh to be genuine except for the Butoh created by Tatsumi Hijikata. However, art must spread its wings once it has come out of the hands of its creator. It naturally evolves over time—like kabuki—which has changed completely since its birth in the Okuni epoch in the Izumo region. If Butoh had stopped progressing after Hijikata's death, it would be a mere fossil today.

Butoh dancers who emigrate abroad often work very hard to settle into the place where they live, plunging into the foreign lifestyle so that their contribution to the evolution of Butoh is visible. I am proud to have contributed to the development of Butoh with several pioneering activities and its diffusion in Europe and the United States. Today there are several Butoh dancers younger than I who produce successful works.

Why has one of the 60s underground movements endured and spread all over the world? It is because Butoh evolves with the experiences and thoughts of all dancers who perpetuate it, even after its founder's death. I therefore suggest that you start training with this book, which is a means to discover this "living Butoh."

Teaching method

When I start my classes in September or on the first day of a workshop, I address participants as follows.

Consider a big fish

This big fish is equal to 1000 hours of lessons in a regular class. Little by little, students eat this big fish and only after several years of work will they absorb it completely. If they miss any classes, they will not be able to swallow some parts of the fish.

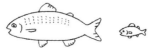

The small fish on the right represents the short-term workshops, which can also be compared to a wine-tasting session where one can quickly learn and gain insight into the various flavors. This book is similar to the small fish, but if used well and accompanied by constant training, the small fish will grow bigger.

With the exception of regular classes, I usually teach within the framework of short-term workshops and master classes. I personally organize these courses for universities, schools, private groups or theaters that ask me to direct. When it comes to university classes, since the students' goal is to earn credits, the effort made by each student is clearly visible in their progress.

One positive aspect of intensive workshops is that all participants begin and end at the same time. This enables them to experience the study program at the same pace. In regular classes, instead, progress is variable since students do not start the work together. However, through constant training and classes, one can work on the same dance and theme taking one's time even for several years. The most important factor is to *integrate the dance training into one's lifestyle.*

If you are studying on your own with this book, you should train constantly, taking your time to do the exercises regularly, either every day or several times per week, even if your time is very limited. Professional practice sees a decrease in quality if basic training is skipped even for just a few days. The body requires more than one trial to retain the lesson. Without persistence, regression is unavoidable.

At present, two regular classes based on the Alishina technique are available: one is at the *Carreau du Temple* located in the third Arrondissement in the heart of Paris, and another takes place in the *Gymnase des Lilas* in the nineteenth Arrondissement, a venue provided by the City of Paris.

Carreau du temple
Photo: Juju Alishina
2015 Paris

Regular courses have taken place since 2001 and bring people together from all over the world, of varying ages and backgrounds. I usually teach in French. However, since I also demonstrate the movements myself, students from other countries can understand and follow the lesson in harmony with the group.

Self-training exercises

If you are or want to become a professional performer, or if you simply wish to reach a higher level, besides taking classes you must train on your own. This book will help you.

For some dances, I rehearse for a performance at least 100 times. This may seem like a lot, but if one rehearses five times per day for 20 days, it is easily done. One must concentrate and improve little by little each time, always trying to progress.

Many people stop training when they manage to dance without making mistakes. I think that only those who reach this point and then start training harder can really achieve perfection. Indeed, besides classes and choreography, basic training is essential.

Do not exclude any part of the body while training

When the body loses its overall balance, not only is health affected, but healthy body parts also lose their strength and efficiency. This is why every part of the body must be trained without exception.

A training program is best divided into two parts. Half of the program should be dedicated to developing one's strengths and the other half to overcoming one's weaknesses. All parts of the body can thus be trained uniformly. To do this, one must objectively know one's own strengths and weaknesses. To this end nothing is better than group training (classes and workshops).

How to assess the quantity of work

Generally speaking, in France, the quantity of work is gauged through the total number of hours done. This seems a logical and fair approach.

For example, by attending a 90-minute class once a week, the quantity of work per year (apart from vacations and public holidays) would be 63 hours. If one attends an intensive workshop for six hours a day for two weeks (12 days), the total quantity would be 70 hours.

In Japan people measure their experience by saying "x years of ballet." The trend is to appraise the quantity of work through the number of years. However, considering that one year of work is very different according to the individual, this method of measurement is more approximate than counting actual hours.

Some people think that the number of hours is not important as long as the result is excellent. They claim that whatever the background, situation or career, the important thing is to produce "quality dance." But what exactly does "quality dance" mean? This is precisely what we will discover together in this book.

USA Butoh Class—Denison University Ohio USA
Photo: Christian Faur 2007

~ Part 1 ~

Body training: basic exercises

Butoh class in Paris
Photo: KOS-CREA 2007

~ 1.1 ~

Seiza, breathing and relaxation technique

Seiza and greeting

I always start and end the class with the *seiza* position and the Japanese greeting (a bow). Wherever we may be, this is basic.

How is the *seiza* position done correctly? Sit with your legs folded onto your bottom, stretch your body as if you were pulling your head towards the sky, concentrate all your force into the *tanden* (the point over the navel in the abdomen), release the tension in your shoulders and ease your breathing. Once you succeed in sitting in *seiza* correctly, bend over deeply, with all your heart, honoring this moment that you are sharing with the master in the same *ba* (place). Never do this in a careless or routine way.

As the saying goes: "When in Rome, do as the Romans do." My daily life is permeated by French customs and traditions. However, during my classes I ask my students, no matter which country they come from, to comply with Japanese customs. The limited time–space dimension of my classes is the "Japanese" dimension, so students can feel as if they were in Japan.

How to stand up straight and sit

If you find it difficult to sit with your legs bent, you can sit in a way that is more comfortable for you. Suffering should be avoided, but at the same time it is important not to give up too soon. If you cannot maintain the position despite your efforts, you can stop. While training, try to gradually increase the amount of time you can sit in this position.

This is the way to stand up in traditional Japanese dance: first raise your heels; then lift your left leg, then the right in order to stand straight with your feet together. To sit, put your right leg back and bend your legs. Now bring your left knee onto the floor then sit on your bottom.

Training can be done by bending your knees and keeping your back straight. The exercise consists of standing up, sitting down and standing up again while balancing a book on one's head. The correct way to stand up may be seen in Part 2, 2.5, *Standing up, walking.*

I will refer to the terms below as follows:

~ *In pairs:* exercise for two people.

~ *Group:* exercise involving more than two people.

~ *Individual/group:* exercise done by the entire group which can also be developed on one's own.

Unless otherwise specified, an exercise is meant to be individual.

Breathing technique

Adult lung capacity is about five liters (1.32 US gallons). However, in the usual breathing process, humans use just a quarter of this capacity. The more nervous or stressed one gets, the more one's breathing capacity diminishes.

When breathing in and out, the human body inhales oxygen and exhales carbon dioxide through blood vessels, which is why breathing is so important. Deep breathing allows for the complete exchange of impure air with fresh air. The following exercises are performed at the beginning of each class.

Candle breathing technique

⊃ After collectively kneeling in *seiza* position, put one index finger in front of your mouth. Now imagine that your finger is a candle and exhale as if you wanted to blow it out.

◌ Now move your index finger away from your mouth and exhale again.

◌ Move your index finger farther away from your mouth, exhale and so on.

◌ You will stretch your arms by repeating this exercise six times.

◌ Put your hands at your sides, breathe in deeply while expanding your chest and exhale, bending your upper body over your knees with your back curved.

◌ Move back to *seiza* position and breathe in as you straighten your torso.

◌ Next, put the other index finger in front of your mouth and, still imagining a candle, blow and move your finger away as described before. Now try to exhale for as long as possible.

◌ Lower your arms keeping them as stretched out as you can, breathe in while expanding your chest and exhale, bending your upper body onto your knees.

Concentrating on breathing is a healthy exercise. In Japan, it is believed that deep breathing increases lifespan. Certain types of yoga consider the ideal exhalation length to be 30 seconds, while in normal breathing it usually does not last more than 20 seconds. Time the maximum duration of your exhalation and try to gradually increase it over time.

Qi (air) change by humming
TRAINING THE CIRCULATION OF QI OVER THE BODY

◌ Inhale, close your mouth and produce a low-pitched hum. Keep the sound constant as if you were reciting the sutras of *Shomyo* (a Buddhist chanting and liturgical praying style). You do not have to croon. The vibration will release your body muscles.

- ○ **Step 1:** Do this exercise while sitting still and plugging your ears with your hands. You will feel the sound going down from your head through your entire body.

- ○ **Step 2:** Lying on your back, continue humming and move your hands away from your ears. Shake your body out and relax all your muscles.

- ○ **Step 3:** Stand up, keep on humming and walk through the training room. Move your body while relaxing your muscles.

- ○ Then do the same exercise by replacing the humming with the voice. It does not matter what kind of voice, just avoid singing or reciting.

- ○ Do the same exercise in three steps: sitting, lying on your back and walking.

Seeing a group of people tossing and turning while randomly crying out is quite strange, as if the training room were becoming a psychiatric hospital. Nonetheless, it is a wonderful show. By repeating this training, one can discover that by moving one part of the body or another, vocal cords open in different ways and free the voice. This exercise is very good for coping with stress.

Socially speaking, it is difficult to walk through a city making animal noises, whereas in the training room this is possible. Shy people, who tend to feel embarrassed, are those who must train the most in order to come out of their shells before advancing to the next steps. You must free yourself at all costs, even if something disorderly or unpleasant to be seen is produced. This work is not meant to be shown, but is made for oneself. If one is unable to succeed fully in this stage of training, the only outcome would be an artificial dance.

TRAINING FOR QI CIRCULATION THROUGH TWO BODIES (IN PAIRS)

- ꙩ Sit opposite your partner. Bring your head next to your partner's head so that your ears are touching (put your right ear against his or her right ear. Then do the same thing with your left ear).

- ꙩ Place the palm of your hand on the ear of your partner. The backs of your hands are touching. Now start humming as you did in the individual exercise: your body will enter into resonance with the body of your partner.

- ꙩ Do the same exercise while leaning head against head, with your bodies facing opposite directions.

Breathing exercises starting from seiza position
EXERCISE 1

- ꙩ Sit in *seiza* position.

- ꙩ Join your hands at chest level.

- ꙩ Lower your hands to the ground.

- ꙩ Open your hands without losing touch with the ground and breathe in.

- ꙩ In exhaling, lie on the ground and bend your body to the right. This exercise is meant to stretch your right arm and shoulder.

- ꙩ Lift yourself up and take up the *seiza* position again.

- ꙩ Repeat the same exercise and lie down by bending your body to the left.

- ꙩ In doing so, you will train your left arm and shoulder.

- If you push your shoulder firmly onto the floor, it will automatically stretch under the weight of your body which is relaxing. This exercise is very pleasant and reminds me of the way my dog lies on the sofa.

- Take the *seiza* position.

- After having done the same exercise, flex your body forwards and bend by exhaling (picture on the right).

- This exercise stretches your arms and shoulders.

EXERCISE 2

- Sit in *seiza*.

- Put your bottom firmly on your heels.

- Raise your bottom and place it first on the right and then on the left foot. At the beginning you can help yourself with your hands.

- Raise your arms and using the upper abdominal muscles, lift up your bottom and put it on your right foot, then the left.

- Make fists as if you were grabbing a stick.

- Just keep your balance without any intention of dancing or expressing anything through the movements of your hands. This creates an elegant movement which allows for the training of the rib (upper abdominal) muscles.

EXERCISE 3

☉   Sit in *seiza*.

☉   Put your hands back and push your pelvis forwards (as if you were being pulled from your navel), as well as your chest and your chin, while bending your back.

☉   Keeping your hands back, put your pelvis back, put your chin back and keep your head straight.

☉   Pressing on your back with your hands, bend backwards.

☉   Repeat this exercise.

Breathing exercise lying on your back
MANJU CONFECTION

The *manju* is a kind of Japanese cake. When it is of high quality, it is wrapped in thin paper.

I usually explain this exercise to my students by showing the gesture of wrapping a round cushion with thin, soft fabric.

☉   Lie down on your back.

☉   Imagine having a big *manju* on your stomach. Wrap it with your arms and legs as if they were thin paper. The more slowly you do this, the more you will develop your abdominal muscles.

☉   Unwrap the paper (your arms and legs) and return onto your back. Keep breathing slowly and quietly, without stopping.

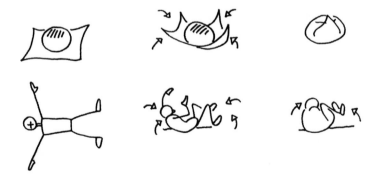

- Wrap up the *manju* with paper (your arms and legs) once again.

- Shake the *manju* from left to right.

- Turn on your left and unfold the paper on your side. Keep your back and your hips bent—this exercise requires back and rib muscles to be flexible. If, at the beginning, you do not succeed in sustaining the body through these muscles, you can use the leg which is on the floor, by bending the knee. Train gradually in order to be able to support your body using only the upper abdominal muscles.

- Wrap the *manju*, lie on your back, unfold the paper (your arms and legs) then lie down again. Repeat the same exercise on the right side.

- When you open the paper, imagine a blooming flower.

This exercise is meant to strengthen abdominals and rib muscles as well as consolidating cervical vertebrae. It is also conceived to develop one's imagination.

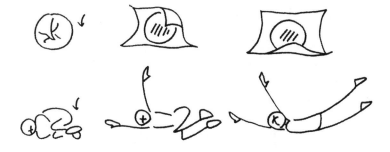

Dry vegetable

↺ Lie down, stretch your arms and legs and breathe in. Curl up by bending your arms and legs, exhale.

↺ You must imagine yourself to be a dry vegetable or piece of seaweed, such as those used to flavor instant noodles when they absorb water. Then stretch your body completely from head to toe. A sensation of freshness will invade your body.

↺ Continue this exercise by curling up and bending only your right arm and leg. Since the right side is contracted, the left is stretched.

↺ Do the same exercise beginning by bending the left side of your body.

Relaxation

- ↺ After these exercises, lie down spreading out your bodyweight evenly.

- ↺ Lie on your back completely still.

- ↺ Feel the weight of your body.

- ↺ Imagine that all body parts are pulled towards the center of the earth.

- ↺ Imagine your bodily weariness disappearing, falling and sinking into the ground and feel your body becoming light.

- ↺ Maintaining this body state, rock slowly. Imagine your body to be a bag filled with water and visualize your bones and viscera floating in this bag. When you rock, the water moves from right to left, top to bottom, giving birth to waves.

To describe this exercise I show my students a supple cloth. I put it on the floor and I shake it. One can also demonstrate what happens by shaking a bag full of water.

In my method, training and breathing techniques invented by my predecessors can be found. Learning such techniques means shortening the time needed to achieve one's objectives by adopting the inventions of our predecessors and by using the information left by specialists. We need to do this since time and energy are limited and we grow weaker and weaker year after year. We would never get to the end if we always started over.

For example, in my class I use the *roku jiketsu yojoho*, a breathing technique inherited from Bareido, the Chinese master of Qi gong who dedicated his whole life to this art. In only 15 minutes, we can take advantage of the results of dozens of years of research.

In the same way, through this book and in only a short amount of time, you can take advantage of a technique that I have developed over 34 years. After this, your turn will come. If new techniques and exercises develop from mine, I would be delighted.

~ 1.2 ~

The back

Exercises to stretch the back

The back is the center of the body. This is why these exercises are so important. The back is also linked to the internal organs, so manipulation of the spine directly influences how they function.

There are several exercises which allow one's spine to stretch—so many, indeed, that one could dedicate an entire course just to this. Some exercises for repositioning and stretching the back are suggested as follows.

Floor exercises

- ꜿ With feet together, lie on your stomach and slowly raise your body while exhaling. Curve your back slightly using all vertebrae, one after the other; tighten your shoulder blades, then release. In doing this, be careful to avoid using only the lumbar vertebrae or curving the back too much.

- ꜿ Advanced students can lift their torso and stretch their arms out fully.

- ꜿ Bend your knees and stretch your back muscles by crouching (see the picture at the top of page 37 on the right). In this position you can massage yourself by hitting your back and pelvis with your fist. I call this position the *escargot* (the snail).

- ꜿ In my daily life, I rest in this position when I feel my back is tired.

◯ Stretch your arms forwards like a cat. Keep your chin, chest and knees on the floor, and lift your pelvis keeping your thighs perpendicular to the floor.

The ability to do this exercise not only depends on the flexibility of the back, but also on its length: those having a longer back will find this exercise easier. Those having a short back will tend to lift the torso together with the pelvis.

Wall exercises

◯ Stand at a wall at an adequate distance. Raise your hands and press them together with your chin and chest against the wall. Keep your legs straight and lower your torso without changing the position of the lower part of your body, curving your back.

◯ When you reach the point where you feel pain, stop in this position. Make a mark on the wall in order to track your progress week after week.

The flexibility of the back and that of the shoulders are two different things. In the exercise illustrated at the bottom of the previous page, it may be that one cannot touch the floor or the wall with the chest because of tightness in the shoulders. In this case, do the exercise releasing the arms.

Ↄ   At an appropriate distance, stand upright with your back to the wall. Lower your arms and put the back of your head against the wall. Bend your head down while bending your knees without changing the position of your feet. The arch in your back should gradually increase. Stop when you start feeling pain and maintain this position for a while.

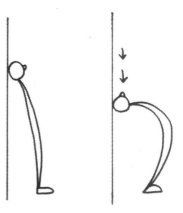

If you do this exercise for a number of years, you will be able to curve your back enough to touch the ground with your head. Make a mark on the wall in order to record your progress.

Curving your back in Uchimata *(sit on knees)*

Elderly Japanese women sit in this position, which is why it is called *obahsan-zuwari* (grandmother sitting).

Ↄ   Before doing this exercise, warm up your knees.

Ↄ   In *seiza*, put your bottom on the floor, between one heel and the other keeping your knees close together. The drawing on the left (page 39) is the position viewed from above.

Ↄ   Bend forwards slightly by curving your back. Then, keeping your knees on the floor and your torso soft, bend backwards. Once the back is entirely on the floor, rest in this position.

- ☻ At the beginning you will feel pain in your knees and thighs, but if you train following the instructions below, the pain will gradually disappear.

- ☻ Staying on your knees, lift the upper part of your body starting from the thighs, while leaning backwards. Train yourself little by little, without straining.

- ☻ Your knees on the floor lift as if you were pulled from your belly forwards and towards the sky (see picture on the right).

- ☻ When the pelvis returns to its regular position, the torso and arms follow. The head is the last part of the body to lift. Try to respect every single stage.

You can ask someone to help you in pressing your knees onto the floor and lifting the pelvis. This exercise is not only meant to stretch the thighs, lower abdomen and spine, but also to lift the internal organs and strengthen digestive functions.

The lobster curve

Traditional Japanese dance *Nihon-Buyoh* includes a position in which one curves one's body backwards starting from the thighs and keeping one's spine straight, as shown by the picture on the next page on the left (page 40). This position is called *Ebi zori* (the lobster curve). It became known through the choreography of *Nihon-Buyoh, Sagi Musume* (*the Heron Maiden*).

This movement was shown in the theater scene of the movie *Memoirs of a Geisha* by Rob Marshall in 2005. Bending backwards is used to express an apex, exaltation and to create an intense dramatic effect, and thus this choreography always evokes acclaim. Learning this position is really worth the effort.

In the picture above right, since the back is curved like an arch, the weight is spread out onto each vertebra. The weight on the knees and thighs is thus relieved. However, it is not possible to curve the back so deeply when wearing a rigid *obi* (Japanese belt for the kimono) or bend the head backwards when wearing a voluminous wig.

In the traditional Japanese dance, when one bends one's head backwards the weight is counterbalanced by the weight of the hair, like a *shishi* (lion). When an acrobatic movement, a dangerous jump or a headstand is planned, a turban is worn instead of a wig.

The picture on page 41 shows the transition from the lobster curve to the back bend. First the pelvis goes back, and then the back curves. This was taken from my choreography *Laughing Fist* from 1995 performed in Tokyo, New York and Paris.

The picture on the bottom of the next page shows an intermediate stage: starting upright, I bend backwards until my hair touches the ground. When wearing a traditional kimono, the obi and the wig, we have to keep our backs straight without arching. However, since I was wearing a soft obi and no wig, I could perform the arch position even when in a kimono.

Photo: Makoto Horiuchi
Dancer: Juju Alishina
2000 Paris

Photo: Christian Faur
Dancer: Juju Alishina
2007 USA

When on stage, one dances for the audience and to showcase the performance. As a consequence, the body in the picture is slightly diagonal and oriented towards the audience. During daily training, however, it is best to do this exercise symmetrically.

There are some other ways to train the back such as the bridge or the arch in yoga. After having done an exercise to curve your back, rest in the snail position, by curling up.

The best way to stretch your back and have fun is to create a human massage device.

The human massage device (in pairs)

ↄ   Work in pairs. One is on all fours and the other lies on him or her crossways. The one who is below massages the back of the other in various ways: pitching, rolling and shaking.

ↄ   This allows the person who is on top to benefit from pleasant stimulation and massage, and, by relaxing all muscles completely and allowing his or her weight to rest on the other, he or she can release all tension.

The picture below shows the same position viewed from the left side.

Do the same exercise exchanging roles.

Please note that changing roles is very important since it allows you to discover what is pleasant for you and to do the same to your partner. Everyone will learn the principle of this mutual massage very quickly.

This exercise is effective both from the physical and the mental point of view, since it allows one to relax and progress while also caring for the well-being of one's partner.

When practicing exercises in pairs or in groups of three, students tend to work with people they know. This can create unpleasant situations. For example, a person who enrolls in a class alone might be neglected; someone might be rejected by the person he or she would like to work with. In addition, when teams are formed by the students themselves, the matching-up process can take much more time. This is why I adopt the following method.

The exercises which can be done only in groups of three or four are practiced only when the total number of people can be divided by three or four.

When there is an odd number of students and an exercise in pairs is planned, I select one to work with me. If there are several volunteers, I select them through the *janken* game (rock, paper, scissors) or I toss a coin. The one who is selected thus becomes the "lucky winner" and not the poor student forced to perform with the teacher for lack of anyone better. This student can benefit from the privilege of receiving instruction directly from the teacher; however, he or she must be patient while the teacher attends to the other students.

When the number of students is even, the master can easily decide who works with whom. Note that the person who decides is the master, not the students. Sometimes the master selects students according to their position in the space. For example: the student who is on the extreme right with the student who is on the extreme left of the room; another example is the person who is the second in line starting from the right with the person who is the second in line starting from the left. Otherwise, depending on the kind of training, I match students according to their height or weight.

As a matter of principle, during regular classes I match those at a higher level or seniors with the beginners. The latter, not being familiar with the technique, will never get the chance to do the exercises properly if they always work with other beginners. Having said that, when one needs to give an example or to develop advanced skills, I match students with others on the same level.

Of course, when several exercises are scheduled, I ensure that students change partners from time to time and that they do not work with the same person all the time.

~ 1.3 ~

Arms, shoulders and neck

Torso work is usually done seated. If you sit cross-legged (*agura*) this work will be easier and last longer. You can adopt either the *kekka fuza* position (a meditation position in Buddhism and yoga—the right leg is on the left thigh, while the left leg is on the right thigh), the *hanka fuza* (only the left leg on the right thigh) or the position in which one brings the soles of one's feet together. People who are not used to this posture tend to lift their knees, as shown in the picture below on the right. Try to bring your knees to the floor gradually.

Straighten your back as if you were pushing the sky with your head (*hyakue*). Imagine that a "skylight" is opening on the top of your head and that you are flying out towards the sky.

The spinning-top (in agura *position)*

While sitting in the *agura* position (cross-legged), move your center of gravity forwards and backwards, left and right, keeping your back straight as if your spine were the axis of a spinning top. Then turn on your sacrum.

Massaging the sacrum seems to have a positive effect on the reproductive organs. First keep your torso straight then release it while paying attention to the movement of the lower part of your body following the relaxation of the torso. The more tension you feel in the first stage, the more you will enjoy the freedom of relaxation in the second stage.

Arms
EXERCISE 1

- ↄ Raise your right arm horizontally and stretch out your hand as if you wanted to reach for something on your right.

- ↄ Do this exercise after having stretched your arms very thoroughly. You must stretch them out horizontally.

- ↄ Do the same exercise with the left arm.

EXERCISE 2

- ↄ Stretch your hands in front of you, at chest level, open and move them as if you were swimming, then bring them back in front of you.

- ↄ The goal is to achieve a sensation of freshness, as if you were actually touching water. Do this exercise slowly and carefully trying to feel the pressure of water on your body in order to soften all the muscles of your arms, from the shoulder blades to the fingers.

I suggest you do this movement in actual water (e.g. at the swimming pool) and remember the sensation in order to use it during training.

Shoulders

With loose shoulders, draw some circles forwards and backwards. First shoulders together, and then alternate.

☉ Lift your shoulders as much as you can, then lower them while gradually exhaling.

☉ Lift your shoulders as much as you can, then lower them all of a sudden, exhaling in one breath.

☉ Lift your shoulders as much as you can, then lower them in three steps, simultaneously exhaling.

Do the exercises above first with both shoulders, then one shoulder at a time.

Do the exercises keeping your muscles relaxed, without forcing them, and keep your back straight. Lower your shoulders as much as you can until you have the impression that, in returning to the regular position, they are pulled from the earth.

The method which involves stopping movement and dividing it into several steps is called "division technique." This is often used in my choreography. If this technique is used during training, it will thus be easier to use when dancing.

The neck

The neck is a delicate part of the body. Never make any sharp movements with it. Gently bend your neck from front to back, right to left. Relax; release the muscles supporting the cervical vertebrae, softly rocking your head right to left. Once your neck muscles are warmed up, do the following exercise.

DEEP STRETCHING OF THE NECK

◯ Leave the cross-legged position and make yourself comfortable. With your right hand, pull your head gently towards the right while stretching your left arm towards the floor. This stretching allows for the loosening of each side of the neck.

◯ Pull your head backwards slightly in order to stretch the muscles at the back of your neck.

◯ Pull your head forwards slightly and stretch the front of your neck. In doing this, you stretch your ribcage too.

If you move the left shoulder while holding your head with the right hand and vice versa, this movement will be even more effective. It is best to breathe in while lifting your shoulder and breathe out while lowering it.

The completion of all these movements requires a certain amount of time. If you cannot do all the movements suggested, stretch your neck as shown in the picture on page 49.

Sitting cross-legged, bring your arms sideways while clenching your fists. At the same time, bend your head to the opposite side in order to stretch the muscles.

Stretching the neck from front to back

◌   Hold the back of your head, pull it forwards and bring it back to stretch the back part of your neck. During this exercise one usually tends to bow forwards bending the torso, while the parts which should be working are the cervical vertebrae. Always be aware of your movements.

◌   Put your hands on the floor behind your back to support your weight and stretch the front of your neck. Close your mouth, grind your teeth and bend the front of your neck. This exercise helps to prevent neck wrinkles.

Lateral movement of the neck: sliding (right and left)

This is a technique used in Indian dance and in South-East Asia.

◌   Move your neck to the left and to the right keeping your head facing forwards. If you are not able to do so, raise your hand with your index finger pointed as shown in the picture on page 50 (center) and bring your head towards it as if you wanted to put your finger into your ear.

◌   You can also join your hands over your head and bring your right cheek towards your right arm as if you were trying to touch your arm with your cheek (see picture on page 50 on the right). You can "slide" your head into the "window" made with your arms. You can see this movement in the Indian Bharatanatyam dance.

At the beginning one tends to move one's neck diagonally as shown in the picture below until one becomes familiar with these movements. However, this is another exercise. When you slide your neck, imagine that you are a papier mâché marionette whose neck is manipulated on the right and on the left.

Neck sliding (front–back)

ↄ   Move your head forwards by helping yourself with the neck, as if you have some ink on your nose and you want to leave a mark on the wall in front of you. Except for the neck, your body must remain motionless.

ↄ   Bring your neck back. In doing so, you will develop a double chin like a turtle. Keep your neck straight without tilting your chin and forehead.

The turtle (dance with the arms, shoulders and neck)

We are now going to do a simple dance using neck and torso movements.

Ɔ Start training by adopting the snail position (see previous section on back training). Imagine having a turtle shell on your back.

Ɔ Maintaining this position, swing your neck gently left and right.

Ɔ Gradually lift your torso and keep swinging the neck left and right while maintaining a regular rhythm. Although at the beginning you will only be able to move the neck, by lifting your torso, you will gradually be able to move more of your body: shoulders, chest and so on. If you lift your torso completely, swing your hands and arms too. Stay in the same place on the floor or on your knees.

Photo: Jean-Claude Flaccomio
Dancer: Juju Alishina
2009 Paris

When your muscles are relaxed, the blood vessels are elastic and circulation improves. During training ensure that you have a bottle of water handy, drink a lot of water and expel waste and toxins by going to the lavatory often.

~ 1.4 ~

The torso, the lower back and the intercostal muscles

The exercises for the torso and the lower back presented in this section are very effective for lower-back pain and for overall health and fitness. Training first one part of the body then another is a technique called "isolation." This technique is included in a great deal of dance and theater methods.

The torso

The torso is the pivotal part of the body. In traditional Japanese dance it is called *shinbo*, meaning "axis of the body." Beginners usually neglect it since they care only about the way they move their arms and legs. However, it is believed that "those who are gifted in dance know how to use their torso." Choreographies which are conceived around the movements of the torso are often the most successful. Thanks to the exercises that follow, you will be able to use every part of your body consciously.

ↄ   Lean your torso forwards and imagine that it is attached to a thread that is being pulled by somebody.

ↄ   Do the same movement backwards, to the left and to the right.

Martha Graham strongly suggested this contraction where the torso is stretched backwards.

↻   Now stretch diagonally, forwards right and left and backwards right and left.

↻   Now draw a circle horizontally with your torso going forwards, to the left, backwards and to the right.

↻   Train by drawing small and big circles, changing the speed of the rotation.

↻   Following the same principle, draw a figure of eight with your torso.

One of the main benefits of this training, when done on a daily basis, is the slimming of the waist.

The hips

↻   Imagine that someone is pulling a thread which is attached to the center of your hips. Now move your hips forwards.

↻   Do the same movement backwards, to the right and to the left.

↻   Draw horizontal circles with the hips linking the movements forwards, backwards, to the left and to the right.

↻   Draw small and big circles with your hips changing the speed of the rotation. Do the same exercise diagonally.

↻   Circles can be drawn horizontally or vertically, working first with one hip and then the other, drawing a figure of eight.

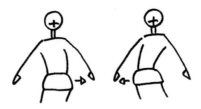

The method involving shifting to the left and to the right using the kick-back of the hips is used in the *Kinkan Shonen* (*The Kumquat Seed*), which is a work created by the *Sankai Juku* Butoh Company.

When doing the exercises described above, focus your attention on the torso or the hips and forget the other parts of your body. They will naturally follow the opposite direction to keep balance with the torso and hips. Draw circles of different sizes. When you draw a big circle, the thigh muscles and abdominals help the movement. To obtain a small circle, you should train the torso and the hips independently. Circles must be drawn smaller and smaller until they become invisible in order to achieve high-level concentration and relaxation.

If you find it difficult to reproduce the sensation of being pulled outwards, try the exercise with somebody moving around you in a circle pulling a rope.

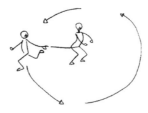

If you are able to move your torso and hips freely, you can do the wave movement more easily. This movement is described in the second part of this book.

These movements come from the *Noguchi Taiso,* which has been integrated with Butoh training. The *Noguchi Taiso* is a type of gymnastics created by Michizo Noguchi.[1] I practiced it starting in 1982 and it was a part of my daily training in the *Byakko-sha*. I had the chance to train with Michizo Noguchi in person, who died in 1998 when he was 83, just when I came to France.

The *Noguchi Taiso* is composed of exercises which were originally soft and agreeable movements complying with the nature of the body. Only after their integration into Butoh in the 70s did these movements became a very hard type of training technique.

One of the reasons for this transformation is that Butoh and *Noguchi Taiso* have two different goals. The goal of the *Noguchi Taiso* has always been to strengthen one's physical fitness, while the goal of Butoh is to create performances. Butoh dancers thus transformed the *Noguchi Taiso* into a training method where movements are geared mainly towards producing performance effects.

This transformation finds its basis within the context in which Butoh developed. At the time of the Japanese economic boom, the keywords were work, fervor and determination. Butoh dancers certainly thought that, for the sake of Butoh development, they should neglect their health and physical equilibrium. After the Japanese speculative bubble burst with the ensuing economic recession in the 90s, people's desires were questioned and certain goals disappeared.

The *Noguchi Taiso* is still taught in Japan by Noguchi's disciples. The privilege of being given instruction directly by Noguchi was a precious experience; in developing my own method I have taken inspiration from his advice.

The movements included in my method are both good for one's health and are beautiful to perform. In other words, I try to achieve the goals of both the *Noguchi Taiso* and of Butoh. Dancers are human beings just like others who must lead a social life. In addition, to be able to dance for as long as possible, it is essential to keep one's body in good condition.

---

1   Michizo Noguchi (1914–1998): Honorary Professor of the Tokyo University of Arts. Founder of the *Noguchi Taiso*. His techniques are used in Butoh and theater training.

When I was a teenager my daily training was very hard and sometimes harmful. I often suffered from knee effusion which had to be treated in hospital. I gradually changed my training and since then I have had no more problems.

Since this book is the result of my personal research, I am sure that this method will not adversely affect your health. However each individual is different: it is extremely important, as Noguchi has stated, to listen to one's own body while training: "Training means fragmenting one's body focusing the attention on the finest differences and reconstructing oneself through the elements just acquired."

Strengthening of intercostal muscles
LIFTING HALF OF THE BODY IN A SITTING POSITION

- ↻ Sit on the floor and raise your feet, flexing them at right angles.

- ↻ Lift your left leg and gluteus and keep them raised.

- ↻ Cross your arms in front and lean your torso to the left.

- ↻ Keep breathing softly while maintaining this position; breathe in deeply, then gently lean your torso to the left and breathe out slowly.

- ↻ Do the same exercise on the right.

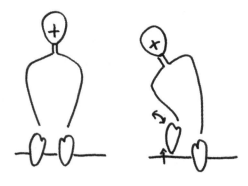

LIFTING HALF OF THE BODY IN THE MERMAID POSITION

Do the same exercise to the left and right in the mermaid position (shifting of the *seiza* position to the side).

Since these movements are of a considerable aesthetic value and allow for the strengthening of the rib muscles as well as for the burning of belly fat, I often use them in my choreographies. The same movement appears in some dances from South-East Asia.

STRETCHING IN GROUPS OF THREE

Three people stand in a line. It is best if they are of the same height and size, but this is not essential.

The person in the middle crosses their arms and holds the opposite hand of the person on either side. The feet of the person who is in the middle must be placed against those of the two external people in order not to slip. Sometimes the two at the sides join their hands behind the back of the person in the center.

The people at the sides take turns pulling the hands of the person in the center. This exercise must first be done without bending one's knees in order to stretch the arms and shoulders. Thereafter, by bending the knees, one can stretch one's entire body: hips, legs and knees.

Repeat the exercise by exchanging roles.

Students who have done this exercise have said that if there were a device made for this, they would immediately buy it. However, a device could not vary the angle of the stretch nor regulate the intensity according to one's condition. Even if it were possible, one could neither press the button nor handle the remote control since one's hands and legs are occupied. Furthermore, the two people at the sides are not there simply to help the person in the middle. They also benefit from the stretching, and thus this exercise is meaningful when done by human beings. Since this work is also very aesthetically pleasing, this is another exercise that I use in my choreographies.

There are many exercises meant to strengthen the rib muscles. For example when we lift our torso or have our legs lying on one side. In my classes I dedicate a lot of time to the specific training of intercostal muscles. These movements are not only useful for dancing; they are also very effective for lower back pain and for staying in shape. I recommend doing these exercises with great care.

Feet, legs and hip joint

The feet

Exercises for the feet must be practiced in each class. Turn your ankles then each toe independently, stretch the Achilles tendon, point and flex your toes, gently tap on the acupuncture point (*tsubo*) called *yusen* which is located on the sole of the foot.[1]

Take off your socks and separate your toes in order to air them. Sometimes I suggest the following game to my students: they form a circle, they pick up a dry cell battery with their toes and then pass it to the person next to them. Toes must be released from shoes from time to time. In western countries people never take off their shoes, even when they are at home. Feet are continuously compressed, except for when bathing and sleeping.

Photo: Nazaré Milheiro
Dancer: Juju Alishina

---

1 On the line between the second and the third toe, one third of the way down the foot starting from the tip going towards the heel.

The legs

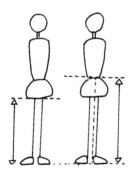

Usually the legs are believed to be the part of the body which is represented in the picture on the left. However, in order to do my exercises, I ask my students to consider their legs as corresponding to the part shown in the picture on the right. Just considering one's legs in this way will have a slimming effect on one's body.

The pelvis has a relevant role in body flexibility. We often think we are lacking in flexibility, but our *body is naturally flexible*. A lack of flexibility only means that the body is not trained on a daily basis. You were certainly able to touch your ears with the tip of your foot or to suck on your toes without any difficulty when you were a baby.

So, instead of thinking that by doing exercises we are trying to make an unyielding body flexible, we must believe that training allows us to progressively recover the original flexibility of the body.

The exercises suggested on the next page are centered on the coxofemoral joint (the hips). Flexibility is essential for a body to be able to dance. All kinds of dances require hip flexibility, both in the East and in the West. I can guarantee that *one can make the hip joint more flexible through regular training regardless of one's age or gender*.

The same cannot be said for other parts of the body (for example, the back, the neck and the shoulders) for which the degree of flexibility does not depend on training. When the hip joint is flexible, one has the impression that one's entire body is flexible even if other parts of the body are not that flexible. As far as my courses are concerned, certain people have gained flexibility in a few months. One should not give up on the idea of having a flexible body even if starting as an adult. Of course, this does not mean that after having gained flexibility one's body will always be flexible. Without training, one's body will rapidly lose flexibility. Constant training and persistence are fundamental.

Exercises with one's legs on the floor

When doing exercises lying on the floor, the back and hips can support the weight of the body so that you can move your legs freely. In my classes I propose several exercises for leg training involving different positions: lying on the floor, on the stomach and on the side. The content changes every time. There is a wide range of exercises for the legs such as: bending one knee and bringing the thigh towards the chest; turning the knees; stretching the groin muscles by opening one's legs outwardly; warming the joint by making large circles with each leg; raising the legs and pulling them diagonally.

Makko ho *stretches (meridian stretches)*

Gym classes in Japanese schools always include stretching exercises called *makko ho*. These are also used by athletes or martial-arts practitioners for their warm-ups. These exercises not only allow for the stretching of leg muscles, they also promote good kidney and urinary tract functions, as well as those of the sexual organs. These exercises are so effective that specific classes are dedicated to them.

If, after several years of training, you are still not able to touch the ground with your head it means that you are not training properly. When *makko ho* exercises are used to warm up for sports, it often takes only one minute or so to be able to touch the ground with one's head. However, in this case, the exercise is interrupted too soon, preventing the body from achieving the quintessence of the movement.

If you do this exercise concentrating your efforts on touching the ground with your head while your pelvis is not correctly oriented as in the first picture, you will feel a certain stiffness and you will obtain no results. There is also an exercise involving bending the back, but its goal is completely different from the one pursued in this section, which is dedicated to the hip joint.

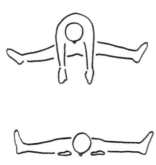

In the first picture, the pelvis forms a right angle with the floor; the navel and pubis are vertical. In the second picture, where the movement is correct, the difference in position is clearly seen: this time the pelvis is bent forwards while the navel and pubis touch the ground.

This exercise is most effective when done at night, before going to bed. After having warmed the body with a bath, take the time to do this while stretching and breathing slowly.

Personally, I often read in this position before going to sleep. Ten minutes is the amount of time generally required for the torso to fall naturally and the stomach to rest on the ground, as shown by the picture in the center on page 63. If you keep reading by pressing down on your elbows, you will quickly want to put your book aside and stretch forwards. At that moment, if you put the inner thighs, the navel, the chest and the jawbone on the floor, meeting your body's needs (as shown in the last picture on the next page), you will be able to rest very comfortably. *This is not a working position but a rest position.*

If you can press your chest down on the floor, sit down on a step of a stairway and put your torso on the step at the lower level leaving your legs and your hips on the upper stair. In other words, there is always a higher level to attain.

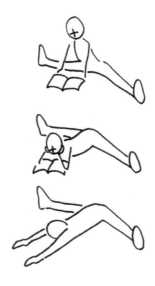

While almost every dance course asks students to stretch the tips of their feet outwardly and stretch out the body, in my method the body is totally at ease and the tips of the feet are completely relaxed. Of course, knees must be stretched. This is the easiest way to do the exercise.

In short, if you listen to your body and you let it go until it rests on the floor, you will be doing this exercise correctly.

If you carry out all exercises fully, whatever kinds they may be, this will give you a sensation of well-being and physical comfort. During training you will certainly experience some difficulties, but if you stop along the way, you will not reap any benefits or real comfort.

When help is required

Warm-up exercises in sports are often done in pairs. For example, one can exert increasing pressure on the back of one's partner to help them stretch. However, people lacking in flexibility usually develop a sort of resistance. This means that the body will refuse to do the movement. The body instinctively does this if it senses danger. In such cases it is better not to force it since it could lead to an accrued tightening or even to a rupture of tendons.

When you do exercises without assistance, you must consider the state of your body and adjust movements according to it. However, you may sometimes feel the need for assistance. In this case, since the body is asking for it, somebody's help will certainly be very effective.

The state of the body changes according to situations. I know that my body tends to contract after a long flight or car ride. I often have to give important performances after long trips of several hours. In addition, where performances abroad are concerned, the body is also subject to jet lag, a stressful factor which is very difficult to overcome. One may thus end up doing the most important things under less than adequate conditions. The ideal thing to do before performing would be to leave the body the time to recover and get used to the new environment. Unfortunately, this implies additional fees for performers' and other team members' accommodation, which are often not affordable.

When I have to dance on the day of my arrival, I am sometimes not able to do certain sequences that I usually do. A low budget actually affects the impact on the stage. Unfortunately, the audience is not always aware of these kinds of difficulties.

Exercises at the barre in classical ballet

Training at the barre or at the floor barre in classical ballet is one of the best ways to loosen the hips.

One must stretch one's leg in a tense posture, by changing position. This method takes a lot of time but since its efficacy is scientifically proven, Butoh groups have adopted it. Considering that there are many manuals and videos on the topic and that there are a lot of courses all over the world, I am not going to talk about specific methods in this book. I will say only that these exercises are very efficacious not only for flexibility, but also for balance.

Shiko[2]

In the kabuki *shiko*, one first bends forwards (as shown in the picture below) then bends one's knees keeping one's hips back. This way of proceeding is similar to the *suriashi* posture in the Noh.

In *matawari*[3] stretching in Butoh and in the *shiko* in *Nogushi Taiso*, the hips are not tilted backwards as in the Noh; the hip balance stays in the center and knees are bent in order to lower the hips as in classical ballet.

---

2   This movement consists of alternatively lifting the legs as high as possible then lowering them by vigorously touching the floor.

3   This exercise consists of doing the splits. The dancer sits on the floor and spreads his or her legs, trying to achieve a 180 degree angle.

Alternatively, you may do the following exercise.

꙳ Stand upright, open your legs, turn your left knee outwards (in the direction of the big toe) and shift your weight to the left following this direction. In classical Japanese dance, this position is called *hidari-kakari* (where *hidari* stands for left, and *kakari* for shifting of the weight).

꙳ Shift the weight onto the right foot (*migi-kakari; migi*: right in Japanese) with the same movements. The hips must always be facing forward.

Another option using the *hidari-kakari* is to turn your torso to the left and stretch the hip joint forwards and backwards. Do the same exercise on the right.

Then, as shown in the picture above on the right, bend the knee fully in order to stretch the legs and hip joint more thoroughly.

The side splits

The side splits can be seen in the French cancan and other dances. In these dance performances the legs are abruptly spread starting from the standing position. However, when doing this exercise, it is best to take your time. Do it gently and carefully.

From the start position of a race, open your legs sliding them forwards and backwards. Fill the space between the floor and your body with several cushions and let your thighs press down on them. By progressively reducing the number of cushions you will be able to finally do the splits.

Some succeed in doing the splits immediately; others can do it only after several weeks or years of training, this pace being very variable. What is certain is that *without a doubt* you will succeed in doing it. If you are in a hurry and you force your body, you risk damaging your joints. It is thus recommended to do this exercise progressively. If you succeed in opening your legs 180 degrees, put some cushions under your feet in order to open your legs more than 180 degrees.

The side splits can apply to numerous figures or dance positions. In the picture below, after having spread my legs, I turn my torso towards the audience. This is one of the scenes from the dance called *Tout l'Or du Ciel* created in Istanbul in 2006. For basic training, you must first learn to spread your legs without turning your hips.

Photo: KOS-CREA/Dancer: Juju Alishina, 2008 Paris

The puppet

This exercise must be done only after a good warm-up.

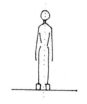

ↄ Stand upright.

ↄ Stand on tiptoe going as high as possible as if you were suspended from above.

ↄ Let yourself fall as if somebody suddenly cut the invisible thread. Bend one leg and stretch the other. Flex your feet. Do not change the position of your torso or head.

ↄ Return to the starting position, following the axis as if you were pulled from above.

ↄ Repeat this exercise switching legs.

ↄ When you get used to the exercise, repeat it again and again in order to obtain a quick up and down movement and vice versa.

~ 1.6 ~

The face

The human face consists of 21 muscles (24 according to the Japanese classification) called mimetic muscles. We do not use them very much in daily life. However, through constant training, these muscles, which usually remain passive, can be awakened, preventing facial skin sagging and wrinkles.

Moreover, the face contains several relevant acupuncture points (*tsubos*). Their stimulation through exercise and massage contributes to overall well-being.

Exercises for the mouth and cheeks
Masseter muscle exercise: chewing gum 1
With your mouth closed, move your face muscles as if you were chewing gum.

Chewing gum 2
Still acting as if you were chewing gum, exaggerate the chewing movement and gradually open your mouth and continue doing the exercise with your mouth open.

Orbicularis oris exercise
This exercise is meant to train the muscles encircling the lips.

ɔ   Close your mouth normally.

- Pucker your lips.

- Close your mouth again.

- Bring your lips in, like a toothless person.

Repeat this exercise until your muscles feel tired.

Buccinators exercise

- Close your mouth.

- Inflate your cheeks by filling your mouth with air.

- Breathe out and deflate your cheeks.

- Repeat the exercise.

Zygomaticus minor exercise

- Close your mouth.

- Pull your mouth upwards in the direction of the right eye.

- Come back to the normal position.

- Pull your mouth upwards in the direction of the left eye.

- Come back to the normal position.

- Repeat the exercise.

These exercises are meant to train the zygomaticus minor muscles which extend along the side of the face from the corner of the eye to the corner of the lips. They prevent cheek wrinkles from developing while pulling the corners of the mouth upwards.

Zygomaticus major exercise

The zygomaticus major muscles, or the smile muscles, are located at the two corners of the mouth. It is best to train them thoroughly. (Note: this exercise must be accomplished symmetrically, without deforming the face.)

- ↄ Close your mouth.

- ↄ With your mouth closed, pull up the corners of the mouth.

- ↄ Open your mouth and smile widely.

- ↄ Close your mouth and keep smiling.

- ↄ Close your mouth normally.

- ↄ With your mouth closed, lower the corners of your mouth as if to form an upsidedown V shape.

- ↄ Repeat this exercise.

These exercises only concern the lower part of the face. However, when students draw up the corners of their mouths, their entire face naturally smiles.

The importance of smiling

When I leave France to go to the United States I am incredibly impressed by the great number of smiling people. No matter who—people talking to customers or managers talking to subordinates—everybody smiles on the job. Even my students immediately show their willingness to build a positive relationship with me in this way. As a consequence, people who do not smile are very easy to detect; they are so distinguishable that I worry about their psychological and moral state. In France smiling is not the norm, while in the United States, for example, when "an angel passes by" people fill in the silence by smiling.

I think that a smile should not be considered hypocritical, a lie or an obligation. By smiling people open up. Similarly, expressions like "I'm glad to see you" or "I had a great time today" are not only part of everyday good manners, they also have a positive effect on the person who uses them.

If one repeats "I don't like it, I don't like it" every day about something that one actually likes, one will end up disgusted by that thing. On the contrary, however, if a mediocre meal is said to be delicious, one will form the impression that the meal really is delicious. Therefore, the use of positive words is thus always better.

Some men constantly say to women "you are always beautiful." Even if they say so to every single woman, these positive words create a relaxed atmosphere and allow the day to go pleasantly.

The Japanese are very reserved, so men paying these kinds of compliments are very rare. Maybe this is because they think that "she will understand without the compliment" or because they are afraid that their compliments would be interpreted as mere flattery. However, I believe that if everybody expressed their feelings with more words and facial expressions, the entire world would be happier.

When my students do a good job or work hard I try to congratulate them immediately. Emphasizing good qualities and showing that you value a person's strengths is essential.

Not only do feelings express themselves through words (or facial expressions) but words (expressions) can give birth to feelings.

The same thing can be said of dance. Classical Japanese dance is tailored in a strictly defined form to which feeling is added. In Butoh the form is often "driven by the heart," but I believe it is good when "the heart is driven by the form."

Nowadays in Japan, smiling is less common than in the United States; however, it is more common than in France. It seems that when Lafcadio Hearn lived in Japan (1890–1904), the smile had a social function. In a chapter entitled *The Japanese smile*, Hearn writes:

> The smile is to be used upon all pleasant occasions, when speaking to a superior or to an equal, and even upon occasions which are not pleasant; it is a part of deportment. The most agreeable face is the smiling face; and to present always the most agreeable face possible to parents, relatives, teachers, friends, well-wishers, is a rule of life. And furthermore, it is a rule of life to turn constantly to the outer world a mien of happiness, to convey to others as far as possible a pleasant impression. [...] Cultivated from childhood as a duty, the smile soon becomes instinctive.[1]

It is believed that habits become second nature. For instance, people working as receptionists in hotels or offices smile as soon as they see

---

1   Hearn, L. (1984) *Glimpses of Unfamiliar Japan*. Tuttle Publishing: North Clarendon, VT.

a client. At first they smile because they think that in order to give a good impression of their company they have to receive customers with a smile, but after a while, as soon as the door opens, they automatically smile, without being conscious of it; it is a conditioned response.

This is also true on stage: when playing the same repertory many times, hearing certain music leads to a conditioned response in the body, face and feelings. For example, even if one is not conscious of doing it, one might lean one's neck to the right and automatically smile when listening to a sound corresponding to a precise passage. This phenomenon is known as *Pavlovian conditioning*.

What is important is that each time one experiences the same emotional state together with the same form. That is because "the heart is driven by the form."

The oui oui[2] *exercise*

This exercise is meant to use the mylohyoid muscle and the digastric muscle more than the other muscles mentioned above.

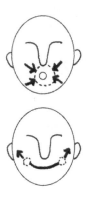

---

2   N.d.T.: *Oui oui* is the French for "yes yes." The pronunciation of "*ou*" is similar to the English "w" sound, while the "*i*" is similar to the English "ee" sound.

Ↄ With your mouth, reproduce the sound "w"—like in *rule*—(u in the International Phonetic Alphabet).[3] Bring your orbicularis oris muscles (muscles around the lips) closer to form a circle.

Ↄ Reproduce the sound "ee"—like in *machine*—(i in the International Phonetic Alphabet). Stretch the zygomaticus major muscles towards the corners of your lips and the buccinators obliquely upwards.

Ↄ After repeating *oui oui* keeping your head straight, repeat it again lifting your chin and looking up to the ceiling. This exercise also trains the mylohyoid muscle, under the chin, and the digastric muscle. This exercise is very efficacious in preventing the development of a double chin.

Ↄ The *oui oui* exercise helps develop a positive attitude. During my classes this exercise always contributes to creating a friendly atmosphere. Actually, even if in pronouncing *oui oui* students do not precisely do the movements as described above, the mere pronouncing of a double "yes" (see footnote 2) allows students in France to adopt the proper state of mind. The technique also includes the *non non* exercise (see Part 2, 2.2).

Exercises for the entire face

Ↄ Relax your face.

Ↄ Make a face concentrating all the parts of your face in the center, as if eating something very sour.

Ↄ Stretch all the parts of your face outwards, with your mouth and eyes completely open. (The exercise is made to work on the stretching or expanding impression.)

---

3   N.d.T.: The International Phonetic Alphabet is an alphabetic system of phonetic notation based primarily on the Latin alphabet. It was devised by the International Phonetic Association as a standardized representation of the sounds of oral language. The IPA is used by lexicographers, foreign language students and teachers, linguists, speech-language pathologists, singers, actors, constructed language creators and translators.

In addition, there are other exercises for facial muscles meant to stretch the chin muscles, move the eyebrows, stretch and contract the forehead, close and release the nostrils and so forth.

The training of the eyes

In the *legong* of Bali (a kind of Balinese dance) or in the Indian Bharatanatyam, the eyes of the dancers are particularly impressive. However, these are not the only dances which integrate eye movement into the choreography.

I compose my choreography in a very detailed way, giving dancers specific indications as to the direction of their gaze. When their eyes wander aimlessly, this gives the performance a sense of banality. The eyes are fundamental when playing dolls or fools.

The goal of the following exercises is to learn to control and master eye movements.

Move your eyes from left to right

I often do this exercise together with the neck sliding (Part 1, 1.3).

Move the eyes from top to bottom

When looking down, sometimes one just moves one's eyes keeping the eyelids open while sometimes eyelids follow the eyeball by dropping down.

Try to look at your nose, towards the center of your face

In some kabuki poses (*mie*[4]) one eye is straight while the other looks at the nose, as shown in the picture below.

Move the eyes diagonally, in a circular way
Nagashi me—flowing gaze

- ꙧ Look diagonally following a trajectory going from the upper left corner to the lower right corner.

- ꙧ Look diagonally following a trajectory going from the upper right corner to the lower left corner.

- ꙧ Look diagonally following a trajectory going from the lower left corner to the upper right corner.

- ꙧ Look diagonally following a trajectory going from the lower right corner to the upper left corner.

One must first train the eyes; then the neck and choreographic figures can be added and associated with eye movements.

Han-gan—*eyes slightly opened*

The eyes slightly opened used in Butoh and that I also use on stage represent the gaze of the Buddha who has reached nirvana or enlightenment. At first glance, it seems that his eyes are closed, but they are not. His gaze is projected a few meters ahead on the floor, but it does not focus on anything specific. Not focusing on anything means focusing on everything.

---

4   The *mie* pose is a technique used in kabuki theater. In scenes where the character's emotions are at their peak, the actor adopts a pose by freezing the movements for a while, staring in front of themselves.

Photo: Hiroyasu Daidoh
Dancer: Juju Alishina
1990 Tokyo

Other eye movements used in Butoh performance

The white of the eye

Roll the eyes back so that the pupils disappear and only the white of the eyes can be seen. This technique was often used in the 70s.

The eyes of the fool

Avoiding focusing your gaze on anything moves the pupils in every direction.

Mirror eyes

Open your eyes wide without focusing on anything. They will look like glass balls or a mirror.

Doll's eyes

The eyes go from totally open to totally shut (passing through half open) according to the level of inclination of the body (see Part 2, 2.7 *The choreography of the doll*).

Following the trajectory of a stone thrown in the air

Imagine that you are picking up a stone and throwing it into the air with one hand and catching it with the other hand, following its trajectory with your eyes. Then imagine that it remains in the air without falling and gaze at this hanging stone.

This kind of gaze in which you follow movements can seem normal, but it creates a strange and subtle effect.

The tongue

The tongue is also part of the body and can be used for dancing just like the other parts of the body. Some Butoh choreographies use the tongue too.

Tongue training

- ↄ The rolled tongue (roll your tongue at the bottom of the palate).

- ↄ The folded tongue (fold your tongue vertically).

- ↄ The pulled-out tongue (stick your tongue out horizontally; it must be hard like a stick).

- The dog tongue (stick your tongue out and release it in order to make it seem as large as possible).

- The chameleon tongue (stick your tongue out and retract it quickly).

Training the tongue by blowing chewing-gum bubbles

- Chew a piece of chewing gum until it becomes very soft.

- Flatten it down with your tongue and stick it under the tongue.

- Make a hole in the center of the chewing gum.

- If you blow, a bubble takes form outside your mouth.

- Blow a bubble, put the chewing gum back in your mouth and chew it again.

I have sometimes spent one hour in class just training my students to do this.

Knotting cherry stems with the tongue

- Eat two cherries with their stems still attached.

- Spit out the pits in order to keep only the stems in your mouth.

- Fold one of the stems and form a circle by placing it on the other.

- Pass the bottom of the other stem through the circle.

- Pull one of the ends holding the other with the teeth.

- Take the stems out of the mouth in order to verify that they are well knotted.

As you can see, there is a lot of choreography using parts of the body which are generally invisible from the outside.

The facial expression on stage

If you can use all the muscles mentioned in the exercises above, you can adopt any facial expression. Your performance face must be different from your everyday face. Even when not wearing a mask, the face must be considered a natural mask.

IMPORTANT POINTS FOR AN ACTOR
ACCORDING TO ZEAMI'S *FUSHIKADEN*

What is important in an actor's portrayal is the similarity of gestures and appearance to those of the character that is being played. As far as facial expression is concerned, it is best for an actor to preserve his natural appearance without adornments, straightforward and natural. (Wilson 2006, pp.74–75)

In my performances sometimes dancers wear masks, but most of the time they just have a thick layer of white make-up. This make-up plays the same role as a mask since it is meant to help the dancer in developing something different from the norm. Therefore, as is true for masks, different emotions can be expressed with some special techniques: *terasu* (expressing joy by bending the head backwards, the face looking upwards), *kumorasu* (expressing sadness by bending the face downwards), *men o kiru* (expressing a strong emotion or rage by suddenly turning the face as if to threaten someone).

Concerning emotion, I leave it up to those who express it. The facial expression should correspond exactly to the circumstances and the emotions that one is trying to convey. In other words: if one is not able to show the expression corresponding to one's feelings, one did not put enough heart and soul into it. The face cannot express an emotion if the emotion is not drawn from some source.

In *The Transmission of Style and the Flower*, Zeami says that insanity (*monogurui*) without a mask or a fake expression is really not beautiful to be seen. The first generation of Butoh purposely emphasized that which was unpleasant to look at.[5] Even today, some people still consider the torsion of the face as being one of Butoh's characteristics.

---

5   Tatsumi Hijikata, founder of Butoh, took inspiration from the works of Francis Bacon to create his choreography.

In the past I trained myself to reproduce this face which characterizes Butoh by trying to perform it on stage. However, this kind of choreography is not appropriate for the works I create which are part of a "New Butoh."

At the beginning of Butoh, the twisted face was not the expression of grief or emotion, but a means to reach other forms of beauty. I no longer use it because I find that there are many other ways to reach other forms of beauty without using ugly faces.

Sometimes my students tell me on the last day of the workshop: "When we have seen pictures or people dancing while dribbling and showing the whites of their eyes, we were afraid that the same would be required of us. But we were relieved to discover that your method was different and we are happy to have had the opportunity to learn your technique."

Unlike Butoh, which suffers from such prejudices, classical Japanese dance has a very good reputation. Learning it allows one to acquire a certain culture, elegant behavior and attitudes as well as the ability to wear a kimono. The introduction of positive aspects of other dances into Butoh is another goal of my method.

Influences and virtues of Butoh

Up until the revolution brought about by Butoh, most dancers had a neutral face. In commercial dance, a beautiful Hollywood smile like in beauty contests is a must. In modern dance, only conventional emotions like ecstasy are expressed. Strong attention has been paid to the body but the face has been neglected.

Butoh, with its choreography showing deformed faces, has had a certain impact and has paved the way for exploration of new techniques for facial expression.

For a long time, comics (hokan[6]) have made audiences laugh through grimaces. Butoh gave them prestige. Nowadays, different facial expressions are used in many contemporary dances and dramas.

---

6   In ancient Japan, a hokan was the male equivalent of a geisha. The hokan used to entertain their clients through their comic actions.

~ 1.7 ~

Hands—fingers

The fingers are covered with thousands of sensitive nerves. It is believed that hands in good health produce an imperceptible vibration releasing a sort of energy. We will train our fingers in order to use them as we please.

In *legong* dance, fingers and toes are arched outward. The deformed body of *legong* dancers releases extraordinary energy. This is the result of conditioning factors like having one's feet bound. We will train our hands and fingers in order to make this a habit, even if we do not obtain the same angle of inclination as the *legong* dancers. The exercises that follow facilitate blood circulation at a peripheral level.

During intensive workshops, I use these exercises as resting activities. There are often also older participants who cannot sustain a frantic rhythm for the whole day. By introducing hand or face exercises, and time for discussion or videos when people are tired, everyone can actively participate in the workshop even if it lasts six hours each day.

Photo: E de' Pazzi
Dancers: Juju Alishina, Ippei Hosaka
2006 Paris

The wrists

- Relax your hands and shake them.

- Clasp your hands together and stretch your fingers.

- Stretch your wrists.

- Take your left hand with your right hand and bend your left wrist bringing the palm of your hand closer to the interior part of the wrist (in other words, stretch the exterior part of the wrist). Do the same exercise with the right hand.

- Bend your left wrist outwards with the right hand. Do the same with the right wrist.

- ⊃ To obtain a deeper curve, put the backs of your hands against the wall; bend the wrists inwards applying pressure with the weight of your body. Keeping the curve, stretch your arms and keep on pushing.

- ⊃ Release.

- ⊃ Repeat this exercise.

- ⊃ If you are used to this exercise, emphasize the curve in order to obtain a more acute angle of the wrist and release.

- ⊃ Repeat this exercise.

This is a method with which I experimented when I was learning the *legong* dance method in Bali.

Dance techniques including movement of the wrists

These are some techniques deriving from classical Japanese dance (*Nihon-Buyoh*). Fingers stay together. This is called *mai no te* (the dancer's hand).

Release the tension when you start moving your hands and recall it when you stop the movement. If your hands are straight, the movement will seem heavy-handed. It is therefore very important to be able to choose the moment at which tension should be released.

Kuneri kote—*waving hands*

- ⊃ Put the back of your left hand under your stretched right hand. The palm of the right hand must be turned up.

- ⊃ Pivot your left hand, turning the palm upwards so that it will end up on the right hand.

- ⊃ Put the back of the right hand under your stretched left hand. The palm of the left hand must be turned up.

◌ Pivot the right hand, turning the palm upwards, so that it will end up on the left hand.

Please note: wrists must always be attached. The leading hand is the one which is underneath.

Kaiguri kote—*pivoting hands*

◌ Put the back of your stretched left hand under the right hand, with the palm turned up.

◌ Pivot the right hand inwards so that it goes under the left hand.

◌ Keep the right hand stretched, free the left hand turning the palm upwards. Join the back of the hands.

◌ Pivot the left hand outwards so that it passes under the right hand.

◌ Keep the left hand stretched, free the right hand turning the palm upwards. Join the back of the hands.

◌ Repeat this movement.

Please note: wrists must always be attached. The leading hand is the one which is above.

The fingers
Exercises aiming at using all the parts of the fingers

The piano (see Part 2, 2.9 *Disassociated movements*)

Exercises aiming at moving the fingers easily

◌ Stretch your arms forwards with the palm of your hands turned up.

◌ Bend the fingers one after another starting from the little finger. Bring the hands back to the chest and open them in one movement, stretching the arms (the back of hands must be turned up).

☽ Bend your fingers one by one starting from the thumb. Bring your hands to your chest and open them in one movement, stretching the arms (the palm of the hands must be turned up).

Exercise for controlling the fingers from their base

I came up with this exercise by observing the training of guitarists and bassists.

☽ Separate the thumb from the palm. The other four fingers must be glued together.

☽ Attach the thumb to the index finger and separate them from the other fingers. The three remaining fingers must remain stuck together.

☽ Stick the thumb, the index finger and the middle finger together and separate them from the other fingers, which remain stuck together.

☽ Divide the little finger from the others, which remain stuck together.

Do this exercise with both hands. If you cannot do it, train by putting your hands on the floor. After having done the exercise on the floor, train without any support.

Exercise for moving the five fingers independently

Keep the five fingers of both hands stuck together.

☽ Leaving the four other fingers together, draw some circles with your thumb.

☽ Do the same with your index finger.

☽ Do the same with your middle finger.

ↄ Do the same with your ring finger.

ↄ Do the same with your little finger.

Be sure not to separate your fingers. It seems that many people have problems with the ring finger and little finger. Some students feel as if they were not dealing with their own fingers. However, if you do this exercise regularly you will succeed.

As mentioned at the beginning of this section, the nerves of the fingers are directly connected to the brain. It is believed that through finger training, cerebral cells can be stimulated and certain brain areas activated.

Dance techniques including wrist and finger movements

When turning the wrists joining the back of hands in classical Japanese dance, fingers are together, while in flamenco and oriental dance they move separately. In Butoh, there is a dance called *ishi no hana* (stone flower) including a movement called *kaiguri kote* which consists of evoking the talons of an eagle using one's fingers and nails.

Ishi no hana training first implies the use of hands, then the torso and finally the whole body.

Ogi tsukai *exercise—movements with the fan*

This exercise is very good training for wrists and fingers. By repeating the movement of turning a fan, it becomes so painful that one wants to cry. This means that the training has been done properly.

Hand evoking the legs of birds and other animals (exercise with the palm downwards)

ↄ *The cat:* form a circle with your hands and bend the fingers towards the palms and the wrists inwards.

ↄ *The fox:* bend your fingers inwards while flattening the back of your hands.

- *The dog:* flatten the back of your hands even more and bend only the first joint of the fingers.

- *The eagle:* open your fingers; fingers are bent like an eagle's claw.

The cat spying a mouse

- "Observe your prey" while joining the hands with fingers bent into circles at chest height.

- Catch this imaginary prey quickly and bring it towards your chest.

- Now, as if nothing had happened, return to the initial position and observe the prey.

- Repeat the movement forwards, to the left (catch the prey with your left hand and come back to the initial position).

- Repeat the same movement forwards, to the right.

- Repeat the same movement towards the left, then towards the right, each time coming back to the frontal position.

- Do these movements to the left and to the right, each time turning your head in the corresponding direction.

Carnivorous plants

Imagine having a bug on the palm of your hand: quickly close the trap to eat up the bug starting from the little finger or move slowly, one finger after another. Do these movements at the same time with both hands. Then alternate hands. Do the *kaiguri kote* movement while putting the wrists together and feel the bug moving across your chest and shoulders. During this exercise, one feels like a carnivorous plant and the face naturally reflects this sensation.

Onigiri *exercise*

Thanks to the influence of Japanese manga, the *onigiri* is now well-known in France. It is a rice ball that is held in one's hands. A rice ball is like a bowl of rice. Since it is very practical to carry and it can be eaten without chopsticks or a container, it is often part of the bento (a packed meal).

Ↄ   Mime the action of holding an *onigiri* in your hands.

Ↄ   Imagine that the *onigiri* progressively grows until it reaches a size which makes you open your hands wide.

This exercise is very effective in training fingers and arms and to acquire a sense of space by progressively increasing the space between the two palms.

~ 1.8 ~

Handstand and headstand

The handstand is a posture which is not used in daily life, and thus it has a spectacular visual effect. It is not only used in rhythmic gymnastics and circus exercises, but also in Butoh and classical Japanese dance. It has been proven that the handstand has physiological virtues so yoga and *Noguchi Taiso* have also adopted it. I introduced the handstand in my classes for performing as well as for health reasons.

Physiological virtues of the handstand/headstand

The handstand allows one's blood to flow throughout the brain, effectively fighting tiredness and weariness, memory loss and mental tension. In the movie inspired by a novel written by Seishi Yokomizo, each time the private detective Kosuke Kindaichi encounters a difficult case, he reflects on it by doing the handstand, which is actually very logical.

In addition, the handstand frees the internal organs from the pressure to which they are constantly subjected and stimulates them. Blood circulation makes the legs lighter, which is very good in cases of circulatory diseases.

When learning how to do the handstand, one should be very careful. If one falls on one's back, even when doing the headstand (*santen toritsu*) one risks damage to the cervical vertebrae. It is there that the nervous system is connected with the medulla oblongata, which constitutes the lower part of the brainstem. The medulla oblongata transmits the orders coming from the brain and it is responsible for breathing and reflex functions. A damaged vertebra can also lead to respiratory difficulties.

In my classes no accidents have ever occurred. Still, during an aikido workshop organized by one of my acquaintances, a student had some respiratory problems and injured his vertebra after a typical aikido fall in which one rolls up on the floor. He was taken away in an ambulance and hospitalized for a time.

Be careful not to get involved in accidents like this. It is fundamental for beginners not to go too fast. First they must gradually acquire the body skills required (muscular power, balance and so forth) through other exercises. People who have already experienced the handstand must not try to surpass their abilities. In addition, the handstand must not be practiced alone. We need an assistant (helper). It requires the presence of two people so we practice in pairs.

Photo: Yasufumi Suzuki
Dancer: Juju Alishina
1994 Tokyo

Using the handstand and headstand on stage

In my choreography I use the headstand (*santen toritsu*). This position can be held for a longer time than the handstand.

I do other things while keeping the headstand position. For instance, one can use one's feet to play with a ball or to click the *getas* (wood-based Japanese footwear) like *hyoshighi*.[1]

To do the headstand (*santen toritsu*) one must hold one's head with one's hands, so that one's bodyweight rests on three points: the head, the hands and the elbows, as shown in the picture below. This position is also practiced in yoga and in the *Noguchi Taiso* discipline.

*Headstand 1—*santen toritsu

꙰ Put your head on the floor.

꙰ Make a triangle with your head and both your elbows.

꙰ Gradually shift your weight towards the back by bringing your legs closer.

꙰ Lift up your legs when you have finally shifted your whole bodyweight.

꙰ Stretch your legs out vertically.

---

1   A simple Japanese musical instrument consisting of two pieces of hardwood or bamboo that are connected by a thin ornamental rope.

This is a movement which can be done only after having warmed up and after having succeeded in putting your head on the floor while keeping your feet on the floor. To start, train against a wall; then gradually move away and try to do it without any support. In this way, you can do this exercise in total safety. The headstand I often use on stage is represented in the picture below.

Headstand 2—santen toritsu

◡ Put your head on the floor. With your hands and your head, form a triangle and gradually shift your weight towards the back in order to shift it vertically onto your head.

◡ Lift up your legs once you have completely shifted the weight of your body. Stretch your legs out vertically.

The advantage of this second version of the headstand is that, after having lifted the knees on the elbows, you can roll out your vertebrae while taking the position.

This allows you to fulfill the first stage completely before starting the second. In addition, since the triangle supporting the body is bigger than the first headstand, it is also more stable (see figure on page 94: the picture on the left shows the triangle in headstand 1, while the picture on the right shows the triangle of headstand 2).

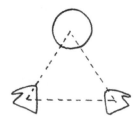

Due to its stability, the second version allows one to hold the position longer while performing another action. It is easy to change the leg choreography, for instance, by opening the legs or moving the ankles. It is also possible to play with a ball using your legs and feet instead of your arms.

The only problem with these two techniques is that, since the head is on the floor, no sophisticated hairdo—wigs, ponytails or any finery whatsoever (which is essential to Japanese dance)—can be used.

The third and fourth versions solve this problem.

Headstand 3—shachihoko[2]

---

2   Imaginary fish. In Japan it has long been considered a benevolent god. It can be seen in the roof adornments on the castles of Osaka and Nagoya.

The picture on the right below represents the peacock pose of hatha yoga. In this position, the body is well-balanced since the elbows are against the chest while the entire weight rests on two points: the hands. Version three shown in the picture below (left) is a more spectacular version of the peacock posture (right).

In this version one's bodyweight rests on three points, the hands and the chin. This allows the legs to be lifted higher, producing a dramatic visual effect.

Since the head does not touch the floor, a wig or an elaborate hairdo can be worn. Even when wearing a traditional Japanese hairdo, one can perform this position.

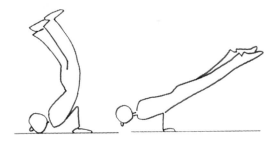

In order to train for the *shachihoko*, I used the three positions that follow.

Lotus headstand

First sit cross-legged. Then put the right leg on the left thigh and the left leg on the right thigh (the lotus position, *kekka-fuza*). In this way, one's legs are seemingly bound together.

Rock the lower part of your body side to side.

Lie down on your stomach while keeping the lotus position with your legs and walk on all fours.

Put your hands on the floor with your fingers towards your legs and your wrists towards your head and keep your elbows attached to your chest. Bend your body and lift your hips while supporting your bodyweight with your hands and your chin. Do this movement while maintaining the lotus position with your legs.

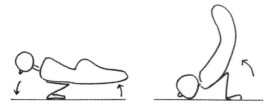

I have used the lotus headstand on stage. However, the visual effect is not the same as the classical headstand, since the height that one can reach is not the same. In addition, the lotus headstand first requires the lotus position to be achieved. Above all, before a great performance, in order to obtain great dramatic effect, it is important not to let the audience see the preparatory stage, giving them a hint as to what is going to happen.

The headstand with three supports and stretched out legs can be done in one second and has the splendor of the *shachihoko*. Personally, I train to do the *shachihoko* in two different ways:

- ꙩ **First method:** roll out your legs starting from the lotus headstand position.

- ꙩ **Second method:** roll out your legs directly.

In the second case, I first trained by putting my torso on the floor and lifting the lower part of my body a little higher each day. However, in this way, one must lift the legs by using muscle strength, risking damage to the lumbar on the way down. So I changed my method. I put the lower part of my body on a bed and I let my torso rest on the floor, training my body to take the *shachihoko* position.

In general, one trains progressively increasing the level of difficulty in order to get to the final achievement. *There is also a method consisting of giving the body the desired shape through assistance which must be gradually reduced.*

The headstand on three supports (*shachihoko*) is seen in the movie *White Nights* (1985) when Mikhail Baryshnikov[3] dances *The Young Man and Death*, choreography by Roland Petit.[4]

In this movie, Baryshnikov shows us two different ways to do this movement: after the handspring (back handspring), a sort of cartwheel with hands and stretched arms, then with the support of a table.

I managed to do this kind of headstand (*shachihoko*) in one way or another in the span of one week, but it was only after years of training that I could do it with ease and satisfaction.

The handstand done with soft legs appears very strange. In the movie *The Inugamy Family* directed by Kon Ichikawa, there is a scene where the legs of a corpse emerge from a lake. When the movie came out, this scene was very controversial. I also trained for this kind of handstand which does not include the use of one's leg muscles, but it is very hard. Actually, when loosening the legs, one's weight rests completely on the head and hands. On the contrary, if one stretches the feet as if they were pulled from above, one does not feel the weight, as if floating in the air and the handstand is then much easier to do.

---

3   Mikhail Baryshnikov was born in 1948 in Riga, Latvia, which at that time was part of the USSR. He studied at the Vaganova School in Leningrad, then he joined the Kirov ballet. In 1974, while on tour in Canada with the Kirov ballet, he defected.

4   Roland Petit (January 13, 1924–July 10, 2011) was a French choreographer and dancer of the opera of Paris. He is the author of famous ballets known as real masterpieces.

I am going to mention a very essential point: some students can do this kind of handstand (*shachihoko*) in only one day, while it took me one week! The reason is very simple: this procedure takes a long time to analyze in order to create a method for each training stage; as a consequence, a non-professional who is carefully learning the development of the entire procedure would be able to achieve the movement of a world-renowned dancer like Baryshnikov in a day. Of course, one supposes that the dancer has already developed the skills required to do this, such as muscle strength and flexibility.

Have you ever tasted a delicious dish at a restaurant and tried to cook it at home? With the recipe, even an amateur can be a great chef in a relatively short time. On the contrary, however, a lot of effort and a great deal of time would be required if one were to try to achieve the same result by identifying the ingredients and the method used starting from the appearance and the taste of the dish. This is why it is so important to learn methods of dance.

Relevant elements in dance instruction

In this section I will deal with several problems that teachers must face while teaching.

Importance of kata (ideal form)

Dance teaching technique as it exists and is practiced both in the West and the East consists of observing and imitating the teacher in order to assimilate perfect movement and form (kata).

However, a new trend has appeared in recent years. Nowadays many teachers declare that there is no point in trying to copy their way of dancing. Everyone should create their own dance. In my opinion this comes from the fact that originality is considered more important than kata, the form. *But are kata and originality really two opposite concepts?*

In this text you will find not only a method to develop your own dance (see Part 2, 2.3) but also a method based on the kata of the movement.

In Japan the word kata is often associated with the words cliché, stereotype or conventional; this leads to a negative perception, as if talking about something which is lacking in life and humanity. Personally, I believe kata holds a more positive connotation.

Let's imagine that your body is cake batter that has been poured into innumerable katas or forms in space. If you can fill a kata perfectly, this means that you have danced well and you have assimilated the sequence. If the kata is original, it will not give birth to something common or conventional. *Learning existing katas is important, but more important is the study of their process of development in order to learn to develop and perform one's own katas.*

My concept of kata is close to the "molding" concept of Michael Chekhov[1]: one shapes the surrounding space like a sculptor, using the body as a chisel; afterwards this form must be filled in with the energy coming from inside so that one gains the ability to shape the body on stage. For more on this topic, please refer to Part 3, 3.1 *Immobility*.

For those who want to get into dance, what is important is not only learning to dance freely and improvising, but also to systematically study katas. As I mentioned before, their importance has been disregarded over recent years.

Increasing one's potential through different types of training

I will now explain the construction of my classes. Since there are many kinds of floor exercises and it is therefore impossible to do them all in a single class, each time only a handful of exercises is selected. Changing the content of each class helps avoid tedium from repetition. Some floor exercises are not mentioned in this book, such as those meant to strengthen the muscles, to work on breathing or some *Taisos*.[2]

After the floor exercises, different standing exercises will be explored, starting from those consisting of loosening the body by shaking the arms and legs, shifting balance, using the arms and legs in full extension and ending with whirling and jumps.

Instead of imposing an exercise on my students, I adopt the technique of improvising some movements that they then reproduce. During my classes I let my body dictate the movements. Since I repeat

---

1   Michael Chekhov was a Russian-American Director. He was born in Russia in 1891. He started his career as an actor, and then he became director of the Moscow Art Theatre with Konstantin Stanislavsky. He died in California in 1955.

2   N.d.T.: *Taiso* (from the Japanese *tai* or "body," and so or "temper," literally "body temper") is a Japanese word used to indicate a practice aiming at strengthening and training the body. In a wider sense, the word can refer to any exercise used to train the body.

these movements several times, my students are able to reproduce them, even if it does not come immediately.

Taking part in the class means bringing one's body into harmony with the teacher's body. Certain things can only be assimilated by attending the class all together, on the spot, breathing the same air as the teacher.

This is why my classes are often attended by students coming not only from all over Europe, but also China, the United States, Brazil and the Middle East. *Dance is a living thing and the interest in taking classes rests in human contact.*

During the standing improvisation training, we discover new movements and often new combinations. Therefore, these exercises are significant not only for the students but for the teachers as well.

If one compares the body and mind to a bank, learning the patterns of the different movements and acquiring the technique is like gaining interest on one's own savings. One can withdraw the money when needed. Like those who have not saved much yet, inexperienced dancers quickly run out of patterns while improvising; they tend to repeat the same movements or move as they usually do. To avoid this, increasing one's savings is very important.

To this end, besides body training, my students also benefit from practical exercises: short choreographies that we call études. Dancing different choreographies allows your savings to be productive and to increase your potential as a dancer.

Just like my choreography,[3] my method has to do with the principles of *kaiseki* cuisine, which is characterized by the preparation of a large variety of small and carefully seasoned dishes with multiple flavors. To define my method, my students often use the adjective "rich."

I believe varied training to be essential for the following reasons:

~ By doing different types of training, you can increase your repertory.

---

[3] One of my performances in New York in 1995 received the following comments: "Other Butoh performances have just one color. The performance by Juju Alishina is multicolored. Moreover her eyes are never flat: they are multifaceted."

~ You can identify which kind of training is better for you and what skills you may be lacking. For whoever is learning dance, the most important thing is self-knowledge.

~ When the training is greatly varied, there is no risk of getting bored even when practicing for many hours and for many years.

Obviously, it is often important to focus on a single type of training for a certain time so that one can deepen one's knowledge of it: without this it is impossible to achieve perfection. Passing from one exercise to another too quickly does not allow one to maintain a high level of concentration. This is another aspect that I consider.

The quality of movement is contagious

I mentioned previously that attending a course means getting into harmony with the teacher's body functions and movement. After years of training with me, sometimes my students naturally learn some movements that I did not deliberately teach them. Some shades of difference which are very difficult to explain verbally such as the balance between tension and loosening or timing and so forth are directly conveyed by the body. *The quality of movement is contagious.* As a consequence, the best way to progress is to afford yourself the opportunity to train with the person you consider to be your model, for as long as possible.

From this point of view, the individual teacher–student learning system in the world of traditional performing arts is coherent. A recurrent refrain is "steal movements from the teacher" without passively waiting for him or her to teach them.

During my classes, when I am at my best and I can show my students some perfectly executed movements, students are also at their best and vice versa. This is a natural principle. Teachers have a great responsibility.

Should teachers do the exercises with their students?

Advantages for students in having a teacher who works with them

Some teachers train their students sitting on a chair, not moving and giving indications through gestures or orally. This kind of teaching is efficient when students are already familiar with the form of movements, as in classical ballet. However, as far as foreign dances (e.g. classical Japanese dance in Europe) or new dances are concerned, is it really possible to train from the beginning without a model?

During a two-week workshop, I had to teach practically without moving since I had had an accident just before the workshop and was injured. Over time I realized that I started to become impatient. Students took longer than usual to understand what to do and they were not precise enough in their movements. Movements were clumsy and the learning process did not develop as planned. My advanced students helped me by demonstrating the different exercises. I think that, without their assistance, I would have had to cancel that workshop.

As I mentioned in the first part, some teachers can convey their dance technique through their body or even through its vibrations. In addition, the fact that teachers and students perspire together creates a sense of solidarity within the group. Even when talking about movements which are somewhat difficult, by looking at the teacher doing these movements with ease, students are encouraged. Finally, when I work with my students, it is easier for me to understand their condition and their weariness; this allows me to plan my lessons appropriately.

Sometimes linguistic problems also exist. When I organized a workshop in Istanbul, not being able to speak Turkish, I did the class in French. In cases like this, both for students or teachers, it is very difficult to convey nuances and fine details. Therefore, the use of the body becomes essential.

Given that I was born and I grew up in Japan, my mother tongue is Japanese. But since I have lived in Paris since 1998 and my husband and his relatives are French, in my daily life I speak French, including with my family and my Franco-Japanese son. I teach in French when in

France, in English in the United States and either French or English in other countries. One cannot learn all the languages in the world.

Advantages for students in not having a teacher do the exercises with them

The teacher can pay more attention to the student's movements since he or she is not involved in doing the exercise. For example, according to the program, this kind of training allows one to correct the student's position, to help them do the exercises or to make them aware of their movements, while moving around them.

Advantages for the teacher in working with students

The teacher surely benefits greatly in this case. No matter how accomplished a teacher may be, his or her skills will decrease if not practiced daily. Self-training requires a lot of discipline and time, hence the interest in training while teaching.

The more a teacher lacks in training, the less he or she will succeed in showing perfect movements to students. Being aware of this and not wanting to bring disgrace upon him or herself, the teacher will gradually reduce his or her movements in class. This vicious cycle must be avoided at all costs.

Advantages for the teacher in not doing the exercises with the students

On the other hand, when one has to teach too many hours, one must think about conserving one's energy. When my day is full—two classes, four hours of rehearsal, social engagements and so on—I try to economize on my movements while teaching.

This is useful when one is getting older or when the student's talent is greater than the teacher's. Choreographers are not supposed to create choreography according to their own physical capabilities, just as teachers should not design their teaching method based solely on their own abilities or condition.

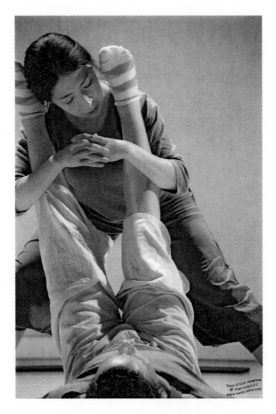

Photo: Jean-Claude Flaccomio
2009 Paris

~ 1.10 ~

Dancing as a professional

Sometimes enthusiastic young students make this wish: "I want to become a professional dancer," or "I want to earn my living through dance." This section presents an overview of the different ways to make this dream come true.

In Japan the word "professional" is often a synonym for quality; achieving a high or advanced level is seen as equating to being a professional. Besides this, what is important is to know if one can earn one's living from dance. Of course, excellence is essential to becoming a professional dancer, but this does not automatically mean that one can earn one's living from dance.

Let's have a look at the different careers which are associated with dance. One should probably consider production jobs along with all other careers associated with dance. Nevertheless, I will focus here on three jobs which are also the ones I have: dance teacher, choreographer and dancer. They are widespread career paths in Europe as well as in the United States and Japan.

Dance teacher

Some people teach dance at university or in dance schools and earn a monthly or biannual salary. Others direct a school or give classes and their income depends on the number of enrollments.

To become a dance teacher one must take an exam either at university or in private or public schools. In France there is the *Diplôme d'État de Professeur de Danse* (State Dance Teacher Certification) with the option for "contemporary dance." As for me, I have a diploma in teaching classical Japanese dance. So far, no certification exists for teaching Butoh.

In the world of contemporary dance or Butoh, professional dancers and choreographers teach their technique or their training method before or after their retirement. Their artistic experience replaces the need for certification or diplomas.

Choreographer

A career as a choreographer consists of creating dance performances and seeing them through to performance on stage. The choreographer's name is always given top billing along with the performance title, which means the choreographer is considered as playing the most important role in the performance. During the performance, several people work on the imaginary world created by the choreographer. The choreographer has great power but also a weighty responsibility. This is especially true for Butoh, where choreographers play the role of producers, directors, designers and principal performers. The choreographer is omnipotent here. Furthermore, in contemporary dance Saburo Teshigawara[1] also deals with stage lighting, scenery and costume design. When one has talent in several subjects, one can become a "one-man band." Sometimes a choreographer works only on films or plays. Sometimes he or she works with a director. In this case, the choreographer comes after the director.

Finding a job as a choreographer is very difficult. I sometimes even wonder whether there is any other career which gives access to so few possibilities. As for cinema or theater directors, it is impossible to find this kind of job through employment centers or advertisements. However, a progressively higher number of young people are attracted by this kind of challenging career, which has become a dream job even for professional dancers.

---

1   Saburo Teshigawara: born in 1953 in Tokyo. He is a Japanese contemporary dance choreographer and set designer.

Choreographer remuneration

When a choreographer is the director of a company, the pay depends on that of the company. Freelance choreographers receive remuneration from their client each time they complete a project. When hired by a theater or a club, one can have a regular salary for the entire length of the contract.

Dancer

Being a professional dancer means giving dance performances. Dancers must understand the performance in which they invest their talent, under the direction of a choreographer.

There is a subtle difference between the work of a choreographer and the work of a dancer. In classical dance, choreographers often instruct dancers with all the details of their choreography, while in contemporary dance they only entrust certain parts to each dancer. In all cases, mastery of both improvisation and choreography is very useful.

Dancer recruitment

~ When hired by a theater or a company, the dancer receives a regular salary.

~ When signing a contract with a performing-arts agent, the dancer receives a fee corresponding to a certain percentage of revenue. Some get paid regularly (e.g. monthly) while others receive a fee depending on the number of performances.

~ Freelance dancers sign a different contract with a company for each new project and are paid according to the number of rehearsals and performances.

~ Depending on the country, some artists can also earn their living by producing street performances. In this case, they get paid by collecting tips.

Job offers for dancers are higher in number than those for choreographers. Dancer recruitment is sometimes carried out through advertisements or employment centers in France.

Let us now consider the current professional condition of these jobs in France, the United States and Japan. In France, being an artist is acknowledged as a fully-fledged job. In Japan, however, there is no way to certify the status of a professional artist. In fact each artist decides, according to his or her own soul and conscience, whether he or she is a "professional."

In France, artists, dancers, choreographers, actors and indeed all performing-arts professionals can receive an allowance and various types of benefits from the government when they are unemployed. However, gaining this status is very difficult. One must meet several requirements, such as landing a minimum number of contracts. In Paris especially, competition is very fierce since the number of artists is larger than the number of opportunities. A work permit is therefore essential for foreigners.

Let us now have a look at the United States. While teaching dance in American universities, I have often regretted that students who have practiced, progressed and acquired remarkable technique did not have any guarantee of becoming professional dancers or indeed of finding a job. We often talk of the "American dream" where everyone's efforts will be rewarded. The reality is completely different: even when one succeeds in becoming a member of a company, despite the unremitting competition, it is impossible to earn one's living without having another part-time job or source of income. Becoming a choreographer seems even more difficult. *As is often true for artists of other disciplines or other athletes, positions are too few compared to the number of candidates: there is no balance between supply and demand in the field of dance.*

When I lived in Japan, until the middle of the 90s, the economy was flourishing and there was a lot of work for dancers. I rarely needed to do other jobs. Nowadays, job opportunities for professional dancers are progressively decreasing and most of them must do another job to get by, as it is in the United States.

On the other hand, amateurs have many more possibilities to dance than in France and one can find a part-time job very easily. As a consequence, if one does not want to earn a living exclusively through dance, the Japanese environment seems to be the more favorable.

Glory and misery of the professional dancer

Dancing is fun and contributes to the beauty of the body and to physical and mental health. However, when one becomes a professional dancer, life is not always simple, but often full of bitterness and difficulties.

In his short story *Odoriko* (*The Dancer*), Nagai Kafu wrote that no matter what job one does, often even the things one did at the beginning with pleasure become annoying; the dream of becoming a star disappears, dancing becomes just a need to achieve on stage.

Dancing which was once part of the *hare* (extraordinary) field passes to the *ke* (ordinary) field once one begins to earn one's living by it.[2]

When one wishes to dedicate one's life to dance, one cannot ignore the financial/material dimension. Besides, one cannot adapt the performance according to the fee. An audience will never understand that a performance is mediocre or of poor quality because the dancers are not being paid fairly. Good or bad conditions are something that must be managed by dancers, not by the audience.

One can keep one's passion for dance unspoiled if it remains a hobby and one does another job.

Even when one succeeds in becoming a professional dancer, life is still difficult. For example, many people are amazed by the fact that the annual income of a world-renowned dancer is much lower than that of the shop owner on the corner. It is not rare for a dance star to live a meager life after his or her retirement. It really is a shame that someone who has talent and beauty, who has become a professional dancer after having overcome many difficulties, having brilliantly succeeded, must end his or her life in this way.

Moreover, in physically demanding professions such as dance or sport, the duration of a career is rather short and sometimes full of interruptions. Of course becoming the best is hard no matter the career, but the fact that a dancer is obliged to retire in his or her thirties or forties and the fact that he or she is physically limited is what characterizes this career, making it different from others. Some dance

---

2   The notion of *hare* and *ke* was formulated by the Japanese ethnographer Kunio Yanagita (1875–1962). This is one of the traditional Japanese visions of the world.

stars have had the opportunity to temporarily live a sumptuous life, but it rarely lasts for a long time.

I remember visiting my mother who was ill in Japan. "I envy you having a job allowing you to work all over the world," my mother declared. I answered back "But mom, my kitchen is a fiery chariot."[3] She seemed to find this rather strange.

I just mentioned the difficult conditions that professional dancers must face. Let us now have a look at their glories. Even if earning one's living by dancing is not a sinecure, there is an abundance of young people wishing to become professional dancers, which shows all the magic of the performing arts.

The satisfaction of being applauded when one ends a performance, while still sweating, the excitement of receiving one's first fee, the feeling of having accomplished something together with the entire team, the pride in being congratulated by the master, the elation of the audience and positive reviews and praise from the press, these are all factors which encourage those who have decided to dedicate themselves to the stage and which are fascinating to those who want to experience these sensations. Most young people tend to believe that youth will last forever. They are not scared by old age, physical pain or instability. Actually, those who worry that much about the future cannot become professional dancers.

This is why it is very important to have a system which supports and educates those who launch themselves into this adventure. Another fundamental factor is the creation of new opportunities. If the labor market develops, competition will be less harsh.

As far as Butoh is concerned, globalization is essential. In recent years I have contributed a lot to this cause, allowing a great number of people from western countries to discover this means of artistic expression.

---

3   "My kitchen is a fiery chariot" is a Japanese expression meaning "All that glitters is not gold," that is to say that despite very impressive appearances, the financial situation is far from ideal.

On the occasion of the Butoh Festival in Paris, the presentation of the following text was met with resounding success.

"You," who are defined (wrapped) by nationality, times, milieu, position and by your own features;

Is this what has defined the self since origin? Where do we find "choice"?

This "body," that you have never had the chance to shun your entire life, this body is also part of the package and defines you.

And the core of this definition is where Butoh comes from, born from a surpassing desire common to all individuals.

This is why Butoh can be acknowledged all over the world and practiced by people of any nationality.

Photo: Minako Ishida
Dancer: Juju Alishina
1993 Tokyo

For a long time it was believed that only Japanese people could dance Butoh. It was believed that Butoh was created by Tatsumi Hijikata for Japanese people whose bodies did not correspond to the criteria of ballet dancers. However, 56 years after the creation of Butoh, the bodies of Japanese people have changed a lot. This may be due to the change in nutritional habits and lifestyle; Japanese youths are taller with longer legs, and their corpulence is actually equal to that of people from the West. Globalization is in progress and not only from a physical point of view, but also at the level of values and meanings. As a consequence one should not state that only the Japanese can dance Butoh, but instead *question the essence of Butoh itself.*

Crossing borders can provide positive outcomes in the long term, not only for dancers who are currently active, but also for future dancers and society. Enlarging the market would involve the "multiplication of loaves" over which people are currently fighting with fervor. Butoh must now involve much more than just a few Japanese people in order to foster its development and guarantee its future.

~ Part 2 ~

Qi training, improvisation

USA Butoh Class—Denison University Ohio USA
Photo: Christian Faur 2007

~ 2.1 ~

Qi training, improvisation

Imagine an invisible hand pulling a thread from the top of your head towards the sky. Your feet are anchored to the floor, linked with the deep core of the earth. Your outstretched hands reach the end of the world. These sensations form the basis of Qi[1] training.

We do not dance alone. We are supported by the Qi surrounding us. An excellent dancer cannot be alone; even when doing a solo on stage, he or she is enveloped by the surrounding Qi until the theater is completely soaked with it.

In my classes, I deal with Qi as something that can be produced, exchanged and received. This part of the training can be considered as the eyes of the "big fish" mentioned at the beginning of this book. You must therefore learn it as best you can.

Learn to tense and release

As Michizo Noguchi told me when he was alive: "releasing the power when one wishes, means submitting the power to our wishes." In other words, learning to release the muscles is as important as learning to stretch them.

---

1   The word Qi (or *Ki* in Japanese) can be translated as breath, energy or spirit.

After having observed different dancers, I realized that the ability to dance or exhibit clumsiness depends on the balance between tension and release.

Below, I will introduce some exercises to learn how to tense and release.

The teacher brings a light, soft fabric to show students how to train by moving their bodies like the fabric.

Tension and release—lying on the back
EXERCISE 1

◗ Lie on your back, breathe, tense up all the muscles in your body and hold the tension for ten seconds.

◗ Release while breathing out. Repeat this exercise several times.

Our daily life is very stressful. Sometimes we are tense even when sleeping. In this case, I suggest you exert great tension then release it all at once, immediately.

EXERCISE 2 (IN PAIRS/INDIVIDUAL)

◗ Lie on the floor and lift up the different parts of the body vertically, then let them fall.

◗ When one lifts and releases a piece of fabric, it falls according to gravity and flattens on the floor. With this image in your head, keep the same position and lift up your shoulders, chest, hips, bottom, knees, chin and head (see picture on page 118) then release and let them fall. This is an exercise of "tension and release" and a stretching exercise at the same time.

◗ Imagine someone pulling you vertically with a thread. I also suggest trying the experience of really being pulled by someone.

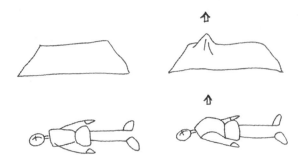

During this exercise, I walk among my students to pull some parts of their bodies. The assistance of a partner allows one to have a better understanding of the exercise.

EXERCISE 3 (IN PAIRS)

ↄ   One of the partners (A) lies on his or her back. The other (B) lifts and shakes their partner's hand, legs and head in order to verify that all tension has gone. Once completely released, these parts fall according to gravity. B must therefore prevent A from being hurt.

ↄ   If A cannot trust B and worries about the fall, he or she cannot release the tension.

Those who see the loosening as something negative would never perform this exercise. Let yourself go like a body floating on the sea.

Stretching and loosening (standing position)
EXERCISE 1

ↄ   Standing upright, go from the tense standing position to total release of the body, then return to the tense standing position. (To know how to stand upright, see Part 2, 2.5 *Standing up, walking.*)

ↄ   Imagine being an inflatable doll and alternating the blown-up stage with deflation.

EXERCISE 2

From the standing position, slowly take the crouching position and then go back to standing.

EXERCISE 3

This training consists of loosening your torso from the lower part of your body and releasing tension.

First do this exercise alone, then in pairs. B moves their partner's torso to verify that it is completely relaxed.

EXERCISE 4

- ◡ While breathing out, move from the upright position to the crouching position while loosening your body. Let your arms and head hang and curve your back (see picture below). Afterwards, while breathing in, stand upright and stretch your entire body. Stand on your heels. With your fingers and toes stretched to their maximum extent, lower your arms and head.

- ◡ Stretch your legs and arms and tighten your entire body. Keep this position for a while.

- ◡ In doing this exercise one must have the impression that the entire body, even the hair, eyes and organs, are tensed up.

- ◡ Go from this position to the crouching position by loosening your body. Repeat the exercise. If you are a beginner, breathe out while crouching and breathe in while standing up.

◯ If you are at an advanced level, breathe in while standing up, then take one breath rapidly while maintaining the standing position. Then breathe out while crouching.

If you are able to stretch and release completely, you can easily do this exercise more than once, since it does not involve a loss of strength. However, if you do this exercise without stretching and releasing completely, it will be painful. You also risk damaging your knees. The exercises proposed in this section consist of knee bends or extensions, starting from tension and release stages. This training is not meant to strengthen the legs or to concentrate all forces there. Other sections will be dedicated to muscle development exercises.

Roll from seiza *position*

We are now going to put the exercises that we have been doing into choreography. I used the following movement in my work "ABSENCE" in 2004. Through this work, Japanese Butoh was officially introduced to New Caledonia for the first time. A part of the performance was broadcast on the national news bulletin.

STAGE 1

◯ Lie on your back and bend your knees. Incline your legs slowly to the right and to the left. Twist your body by turning your torso in the opposite direction to the lower part of your body, then release. This simple movement allows the pelvis to come back into place.

◯ Afterwards tilt your legs to the right. After having stretched your legs, twist your torso to the right, following the movement of the legs.

◯ Rest on your right side in the fetal position.

◯ Bring your legs to the left to go back to the initial position, that is to say, lying on your back with your knees bent.

🜂   Do the same exercise on the left.

🜂   Imagine that your weight passes from one side to the other, making you tilt to either side.

When you tilt your legs to the right, your torso naturally tends to go to the right too. When the torso naturally bends on the same side as the lower part of the body and you release your body, this automatically creates a sense of satisfaction. Every now and then, letting our body talk is very useful. Let your body go in the direction that it desires. If you feel any discomfort this means that you are not completely relaxed. You could have unusual tension in some parts of your body or some other issues.

STAGE 2

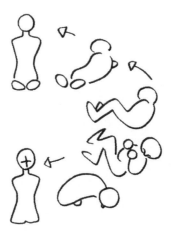

🜂   Lying on your back, bend your knees, lift your legs and bend your hands and head inwards as in the fetal position. The bodyweight shifts to the right side so that you fall to the right; now roll up into a ball.

◌ Without loosening your body (as in Stage 1) stays in the fetal position and shift your bodyweight into your pelvis and legs. Consequently, the torso straightens up like a standing doll and you end up in the *seiza* position, your arms naturally hanging from the shoulders.

◌ Your weight shifts into the torso towards the right. Your bottom rolls onto the floor. Your weight shifts towards the center of the body and you come back to the initial position, lying on your back. Then the weight goes to the left, you fall onto this side to go into the *seiza* position.

◌ Do all these movements slowly, with care and possibly with ease.

STAGE 3

Start in the fetal position lying on your back and let the Qi pass first through the right side of the body. Rise up in order to go back onto your knees. At this moment the Qi moves through the body and goes towards the sky starting from the tip of the right hand.

STAGE 4

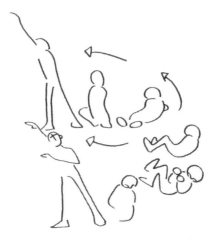

This is the same movement as in Stage 3, but before going to the right and left you have to stand up. Your body is therefore completely stretched.

Effects: by practicing this, you will use your energy efficiently, you will feel less tired, have solid abdominal muscles and feel less heavy and more energetic. Have you ever felt the need to sustain your body with the arms while getting up, because you were tired? If that happens, remember these exercises and you will be able to move more freely and elegantly.

Flower—side loosening
STAGE 1

Stand with your legs shoulder-width apart. Spread your bodyweight on both feet. Then shift the weight onto just one foot. When you do so, your body bends to one side and your arms naturally hang vertically to the floor. Relax your knees. Let your head fall onto your shoulders while holding your gaze forwards. This exercise is meant to stretch the lateral muscles to their maximum extent.

Now imagine that the liquid contained in your body is pouring towards the center in order to go back to a straight standing position on two feet. Then "pour" your bodyweight onto the other side.

STAGE 2

Let's say we start from the left. From the standing position, shift your weight to the left, as in the previous exercise. Think of your body as empty. The body, bent towards the left, is completely relaxed and the neck and the arms rock gently.

The earth's energy enters your body starting from the left foot. The energy traverses the body diagonally in order to move towards the sky.

The body, deprived of energy, falls horizontally onto the right side. The energy of the earth enters from the right foot, crosses the entire body obliquely and spreads towards the sky from the left hand.

Imagine this: a doll inflated with air like a balloon becomes completely floppy once deflated. But it takes form little by little according to its inflation in order to get back to its original shape.

Look carefully at the second picture. The correct movement is indicated by the arrows. What you can see on the right is instead a bad example. Stretch the side well and bend it without twisting.

HOW TO BREATHE WHILE DOING THIS EXERCISE:

Breathe in when the earth energy crosses your body diagonally. Breathe out, audibly, in a single breath while transmitting the energy from the left hand towards the sky. Breathe in when the body falls and breathe out by releasing so that the torso dangles to the side.

This exercise is based on one of the exercises that I used to practice in the *Byakko-sha* Butoh group at the beginning of the 80s.

Seasons (individual/group)—*application of these exercises to longer choreographies*

THE PLANT CYCLE

Now let's do a mixed exercise called the seasons. This choreography evokes several things at once: the four seasons, the life of man and plants.

Start from lying on your back, lift up by curving your back and straighten until you are upright. Then let your body fall like a withering plant, to come back to the initial position, on your back.

The master explains this movement by comparing the body with a piece of fabric.

He or she shows the students the following: after having rolled a piece of fabric on the floor, he or she picks it up until it hangs vertically in order to finally let it softly fall to the floor. After this demonstration, the master does the movements as an example for students.

THREE ELEMENTS

- *The seasons:* spring, summer, autumn, winter.

- *The life of man:* fetus, baby, child, teenager, adult, old age, death.

- *Plants:* the earth, the seed (bulb), sprouting, the plant's death and return to the earth.

Choreography

- Lie on your back like a corpse. Imagine that your body is a flat surface.

- Underground, the magma boils and the earth starts to quake. Use all parts of the body with no exception. On this occasion, take advantage of the exercises that we have practiced at the beginning of this section.

- Curl up on your side in the fetal position.

- Spring comes and the trees bud.

- Plants grow (baby).

- They grow quickly and develop more and more (childhood).

- Beginning of summer: buds (adolescence).

- Full summer. Flowers in full bloom (adult). Everyone can choose a flower. Lift the fabric up and stretch it well.

- End of summer. The flower starts to wither (maturity).

- Autumn arrives and the flowers wither. The shape shrinks and curves due to age. The fabric softly falls.

- End of autumn (old age). The end of life comes closer.

- Winter (death). Curl up. Lie on your back with arms and legs unfolded. The fabric once again lies flat.

Note: When practicing in a group, make sure that the speed of all participants is almost the same. In order to reach the climax points together (e.g. full summer and death), everyone must try to regulate their speed with others.

Especially when standing up, the movement tends to lose precision. Practice this taking all the time you need.

In order to develop harmonious movements, train the smaller muscles and carefully control the movement of your body.

In the arts, the definitions, laws and cycles of nature are often integrated into works conceptually. Since these elements possess a clear and universal logic, they are easily understandable all over the world.

I created this lesson from one given by Semimaru, a member of *Sankai Juku*, on the occasion of his workshop in 1992. This is one of my most appreciated lessons since it allows the use of the entire body as well as one's imagination, and gives everyone a degree of creative freedom.

~ 2.2 ~

Waving

At the beginning of this session, the teacher shows the students a piece of soft, light fabric which represents a body in order to show them how the waves (movements of the fabric) move across the fabric from one end to the other.

When one takes one end of the fabric and shakes it softly, the input (information) is conveyed to the other end through the waves that follow the movement.

If one does the same thing using stiff fabric or paper, the waves do not flow in the same way. Therefore, you can easily understand how important softening the body through constant training can be.

Wave game (group)
STAGE 1

Stand in a circle facing your partners and hold hands with the people beside you. At the beginning, time is dedicated to transmitting energy like in a Japanese game called *shin-gen-chi*: if the person on your right squeezes your right hand, you have to squeeze the right hand of the person on your left with your left hand. By squeezing the right hand of that person, you are conveying an input. At this precise moment you can change direction and speed. In this game, the one playing "the cat" is in the middle of the circle and must guess where the input is.

This activity allows one to evaluate the spirit of cooperation between participants. I propose this activity to my students on the first or second day of my workshop. It is a child's game, but it is not always as easy as it seems. Participants often cannot move past this and run out of time for other exercises. But in most cases, the students who have little difficulty show enthusiasm and have fun and can train effectively right up until the last day. The most common mistakes are the following: instead of a single input, often there is more than one, or the input simply gets lost somewhere. This happens when someone grasps two hands at the same time or squeezes the hand of the next person exerting pressure which is too weak to be perceived by the other.

STAGE 2

Form a circle. Swing your arms while holding the hands of the people next to you, feeling their movements. At the beginning, move your arms together, and then create a wave by swinging the arms in turn.

If you lower your arms with force, your neighbor will feel the wave entering his or her body better.

STAGE 3

Sit down, let the wave enter from the right hand, crossing the body and coming out of the left hand. Each person expresses this phenomenon with their body and conveys it to the person next to them. The master shows how the wave moves through each part of the body.

The wave which has entered through the tip of the fingers crosses the body—starting from the wrist, the elbow, the shoulder, the shoulder blade and so on—then goes forwards and backwards, to the right and to the left, upwards and downwards, sliding over the skin. The body just has to obediently respond to the wave movement. You will move all the parts of your body that you can such as your chest, neck, chin, head and eyeballs. Finally the wave starts from the other arm and it is conveyed to your neighbor through the fingers.

STAGE 4

This is the same activity as in Stage 3 but in a standing position. In this position you can use your entire body. In this way, the wave is amplified. Forming a circle, move your body without changing your place.

At the beginning, while seated, use just the upper part of your body. Next transmit the wave to your entire body by standing up.

You might already have seen this technique in hip-hop or break-dance. Here you should not be so concerned with the aesthetics of the movement, rather focus on conveying the waving movement to the person next to you.

Moving by visualizing the wave position is more difficult than you think. If one is not careful, one can give the impression of being limp. Therefore, do the following exercises with help from a partner.

The bug crawling along the body (in pairs)

Remember the image of the wave moving through the soft, light fabric. If you are a teacher, remind your students of this and do not hesitate to show them it again. Demonstrating the example to students on several occasions is very helpful, until they completely soak up the vision and the physical sensation. When all participants have understood the exercise, have them work in pairs. At this moment, choose an assistant or one of your students.

One of the partners becomes the "guide" (the one giving input to the movement—G) and the other is the "follower" (the one receiving the input—F).

F stands with their legs slightly more than shoulder-width apart and raises their arms horizontally.

G gives F a weak input (information) with their fingertip: the bug moves onto the right hand of F, crawls across the body and leaves from the left hand.

Stimulate only one point at time.

In stage 1, F concentrates only on the parts of the body where the bug is crawling, without moving.

In stage 2, F waves the parts of the body where the bug is moving.

Work on this movement in turn. Try it on the different parts of your body.

Often some students complete this activity much sooner than others and seem bored while waiting. Others are much slower.

Participants should therefore be aware of what is going on around them during these exercises. If you feel like you are finishing later than most, hurry up. If you are too fast, slow down.

For those who finish before the others, it could be useful for the teacher to give them an optional activity, something easy that can be understood even at a distance.

The teacher must impose his or her directives even if students already know the exercises from other workshops. The work can be similar, but the process varies subtly according to the teacher. It is self-evident that each student cannot act or do as they please. After having worked in pairs, train without assistance.

Non non (no no) exercise—vibration

When the body waves at its fullest ability, a vibration develops. If you can do this movement well, you will feel your skin and flesh trembling and almost splitting from the bones.

- Shake your body to the right and to the left, like a little child saying "no, no" through gestures.

- Intensify these movements.

- Increase the frequency of these movements on the right and left while reducing their extent.

- Stop wriggling your body and keep trembling while looking forwards. Be sure that the vibration reaches all body parts.

- Reduce the vibration in order to halt little by little.

Education and societal constraints drive people in modern society to withhold or suppress emotions. Actually, emotions are rarely so deep as to give birth to vibrations.

However, this vibration is sometimes needed on stage. Directors or choreographers will simply say to dancers "vibrate," but they never teach them how to do it. The vibration technique must therefore be learned. This is not a difficult technique. Some can do it immediately, while others cannot, even after years of practice. As for me, it took me several years to learn how to vibrate properly. In any case, this comes suddenly once one finds the secret. Therefore, keep training patiently.

The *non non* method aside, there are other techniques such as shaking the knees nervously or carrying a bell.

In my method, there is also the *oui oui* exercise (See Part 1, 1.6).

Now let's apply the wave movement to the choreography that we have just learned.

The invisible cushion (in pairs)

Choose a partner who is about the same size as you. Put your back firmly against theirs. Carefully explore the back of your partner going from side to side. If the pressure is uniformly shared, you will be able to stand up and sit down without using your hands.

Then, with your partner, perform the following movements: your back separates from your partner's back when pushed, then joins the other's back again as if pulled by a magnet. Focus your attention on the feeling in your back.

Then, imagine that between your back and your partner's back there is an invisible cushion and perform the same movements without touching your partner's back.

In the *Nihon-Buyoh* repertory (traditional Japanese dance) there is a technique called *sezuri* where a man and a women express their love while being back to back. In reality, they cannot touch backs because of the obi, the traditional belt. However, they dance imagining that their backs are touching. This is the same movement represented in the picture above, with the invisible cushion placed between the two dancers.

To reflect each and every position of your partner, relax your knees, head, neck—all the parts of your body—and let your back be the driving force. Let your arms hang and wave forwards, to the side and upwards.

Coral (group)

Gather together with your backs facing the center of the group. Since it is difficult and possibly dangerous to touch backs with all the others, imagine that an invisible cushion is placed in the middle of the circle among the different people. Push each other: from time to time you will be ejected from the circle to return into it. Repeat these movements. With arms and neck going out of the circle in all directions, rock your body like seaweed in the sea. Release, your knees bending. Avoid sitting heavily: keep waving and make sure that you can recover immediately.

All those who are making the group turn and change direction, train their arms like *koinoboris*.[1]

Keep your eyes half-closed (*han-gan*). Do not close them completely (see Part 1, 1.6 *The face*).

Looking around you, move so that the mass of people can find its own harmony. For example, if your neighbors stand up next to you, sit or bend over. If they hold a low position, stand up. By making up for what is missing and containing what is excessive, *each person is responsible for the entire group and its shape*.

When this method works and everybody is in harmony with others, one can feel it and it is very pleasant for dancers and the audience. This creates more motivation to keep swinging, swaying and moving with the wave. Music can therefore amplify this symbiotic moment.

---

1   The *koinoboris* are koi carp-shaped wind socks that flow in Japan to celebrate *Tango no Sekku*, a traditional event which is now a designated national holiday and the *Kodomo no hi*, Children's Day.

Butoh class in Paris
Photo: KOS-CREA 2007

~ 2.3 ~

About improvisation

In a constantly changing world, it is important to be able to *find pertinent answers quickly*. Although we can control ourselves, it is impossible to control the surrounding environment. Even if, after several years, we are able to solve a problem, the situation will most likely have changed in the meantime.

If one considers that, in choreography, movements are generally planned, improvisation is different since one dances and thinks at the same time.

What distinguishes improvisation from choreography?

When comparing an improvisation that was created in a few seconds with choreography that required three months of preparation, can one really say that the only difference lies in the preparation time?

Real improvisation is something that comes to life in a few seconds; it is not a simple rearrangement of previously assimilated information or a performance of previously learned choreography. Learning choreography means assimilating something which comes from outside and applying a series of modifications; however, our body already presents a series of different movements and forms and improvisation means taking advantage of them. Oriental medicine deserves a mention here, since its principle is stimulating natural healing power just like improvisation is meant to stimulate natural dancing power.

The inner and external action

Choreography is designed by a choreographer. It is a series of instructions and directives that dancers must interiorize. However, improvisation is determined by the outside; it is influenced by the situation, other dancers, the audience and the surroundings.

Does improvisation require a basis?

Quality considerations aside, everyone can dance, given that everyone has a body with which to move. Even true beginners who have never learned how to dance can produce something, if required. Generally, everyone walks, sits down, lies down and can stretch their arms upwards in everyday life. Moreover, most people who have attended school have already practiced some physical activities or sports.

Feldenkrais[1] says that if one takes a person who cannot play the piano and leaves them in front of a piano for an entire day, they will try to reproduce some sounds making innumerable attempts and mistakes. After a while, they will find some relationships between the keys and finally succeed in playing a simple piece at the end of the day.

Even people who have never danced can produce something if they work with their body over the course of a day.

Nevertheless if one moves freely, one will also feel the need to learn more about movements. Indeed when one moves with no knowledge, usually one has a tendency to repeat the same movements. This is the moment at which one may wish to learn new movements and combinations.

In Butoh there is a branch focusing on improvisation and another on form. In recent years the improvisation branch has become the main wave, so much so that certain people consider Butoh part of a range of improvisation techniques.

Those preferring improvisation are often people who are tired of rules imposed by dance such as ballet or are people who are not able to follow these rules. However, my opinion is that improvisation is far from

---

1   Moshe Feldenkrais (1904–1984) was a physicist born in the Russian Empire and creator of the Feldenkrais method.

easy. Freedom is challenging. Everything becomes our responsibility and we must constantly think about what will come next.

Dancing to set choreography is easier since movements are completely assimilated by the body. Of course, this process takes more time.

Jam session (session of dance improvisation)

Originally a jam session was a musical performance improvised by jazz musicians that did not address an audience. It was created to share the pleasure of playing and for musical research. Many jazz musicians love the freedom of playing in jam sessions after having worked in clubs. On stage a repertory of standard jazz is required. But in a jam session, one can ignore this rule and feel completely free. The jam serves as a kind of release.

Moreover, this method is also very effective in forming a group. By organizing a jam session on their first meeting, musicians can understand their level of compatibility.

Personally, I used to play several instruments until I was 17 and I participated in several jams. Therefore I am very familiar with the excitement and pleasure of improvisation. One starts by proposing a theme to which others answer and so on. The contribution of each musician creates a global vibration which becomes progressively stronger. Participants acquire a mental state which is most suitable for musical research.

General improvisation practice in dance is a newer concept than in music.

Nowadays the jam session in dance improvisation is practiced everywhere. I have also proposed numerous jam sessions on some of my courses, in particular in 2004.

Since the jam session cannot be considered a proper class, I charged half the fee for a normal class. In some jam sessions that I propose, students just dance for one hour. They can sit and rest if they are tired, they can dance with others or alone. However, disturbing others and talking is forbidden. The jam master takes responsibility for the music and sometimes participates in the jam.

If you take part in several jams you will be able to do longer improvisations. I noticed a considerable difference between the students enrolled in the jam session class and those who were not.

When students take part in a one-hour jam session, some get bored. They do not know what to do or they feel abandoned by the teacher. Then they start thinking "I don't know why I'm here"; "I want to go home." No, this kind of job cannot be done at home: unless someone suggests and forces you to do so, it is difficult to be successful in improvising alone.

For many reasons, dance is freer than music. In musical jams people are rarely at a loss for what to do. Even when dealing with improvisation, a musician cannot play just anything: a theme and a key have been decided before starting. In addition, there is another rule: regularly return to the theme so that you can develop other parts of the same theme freely.

This "freedom with constraints" is easier to manage than total freedom.

Those performing choreography can be compared to employees, and those improvising to the unemployed. Even when the latter have some spare time they do not enjoy the pleasure of being on holiday: they keep worrying about how to get by. Between one group and the other we can place freelance workers. They are flexible and can have spare time even when working. This is what we mean by "improvisation with constraints."

The jam with constraints corresponds to contact improvisation. Since the latter has been linked to Butoh since the 90s, I will also discuss it.

Personally, what I find interesting about improvisation is chance and speed. New things occur by chance and this process is usually extremely rapid. The picture at the top of page 142 was taken during one of my workshops while the one on the bottom was taken during a performance. In each of them, the photographer captured an improvised movement, that is to say that combinations were not planned, but were partly created by chance.

Photo: Camille Perrière
Dancers: Peggy Gilardi, Juju Alishina
2003 Paris

"Absence"
Photo: Frédéric Thérisod
Dancers: Ippei Hosaka, Juju Alishina
2005 New Caledonia

Contact improvisation comes from modern dance and belongs to the twentieth-century modern-art movement. It has evolved around Steve Paxton in the United States since the 60s. It was thus a product of the same era as Butoh, but as contact improvisation started gaining popularity and renown in Japan only in the 90s, this method was not used in the first Butoh training sessions. It does have some things in common with Butoh from the social movement point of view. For example, its members live in communities. In the 80s, several contact improvisation communities dissolved, as did Butoh communities. Furthermore, from a technical point of view, contact improvisation uses the Qi and bodyweight shifting. These features connect this improvisation with my method, and I integrate the contact improvisation method into my training program.

We learn contact improvisation in Part 2, 2.4. In a jam you must change partners during training. Training with several people is fundamental. As in martial arts, you react differently according to your partner and this requires learning and training.

Among the participants of my workshops, there are often dance teachers, university teachers or organization managers. I met a woman who organized and managed contact improvisation in Pennsylvania. She had also noticed the existence of common points between contact improvisation and Butoh. She appreciated my program very much. She sometimes organizes jams with 200 people. It must really be wonderful to jam with so many people!

I think that nowadays all dancers have experience in contact improvisation. It is the same for choreographers, who use it both for training and choreography. Even when it is not used consciously, it seems that contact improvisation has really penetrated the dance world even if one does not necessarily realize it.

Those who have problems dealing with people from different backgrounds and social milieux will find contact improvisation very hard since one's body "melds" with a stranger's body. Sometimes it seems like people have ended up at a partner-swapping party and are trying to escape from this situation. However, in France, jams are well-regulated and do not imply any kind of danger. It is a simple question of routine. Of course, if you do not like your partner, you can change.

In general, the Japanese have little physical contact with people. Mostly they greet one other from a distance even within their own family. There's no physical contact once one has become an adult. When I went back to Japan in 2001, my parents came to pick me up at the airport. My husband (who is French) was then surprised and said "how come even after such a long separation you don't shake hands or hug and kiss?"

When I first came to Paris in the beginning of the 80s, I found the way people kiss in the street really exotic. Even though young people nowadays in Japan are more outgoing than before, it is still rare for an old couple to show their feelings in public. This lack of physical contact could be the cause of deviant behaviors like groping people on the metro. However, contact improvisation currently is well-known and popular in Japan and I think that this is a very positive thing.

After having participated in some workshops and jam sessions, I see the advantages in improvisation. In a regular class, the differences in skill levels between participants is blatant. In contact improvisation, this difference is less evident and beginners or participants who are not yet that skilled can still have fun.

When one improvises completely, progress is usually really slow. But when freedom is channeled in a certain way by a number of directions, one can create something valid both for dancers and the audience.

At the beginning, jams were meant for the dancers themselves and they were not meant to become a show. Contact improvisation was an experiment to try to create something within a community from the counterculture. Little by little, however, the jam has started being shown to the audience.

When speaking of a "jam with constraints," one may think of ballroom dancing. But the term jam cannot be applied to the latter. In addition, the spirit of people who love to jam is really different from that of lovers of ballroom dance.

In these kinds of dances, you improvise according to your partner; you just have to understand the steps and combinations to do by listening to the music and applying them. So the mambo, cha-cha-cha, Cuban rumba, waltz and tango all have their own rules.

In ballroom dance, the couple is usually a man and a woman and the man leads, while the woman is the leader's partner. In a dance jam session, a woman can lead a man and a couple can be formed by two people of the same sex. When I lived in Japan, I also studied ballroom dances for a while. Since they are really rich in combination techniques, I still use them to create my dances.

The figure lift

The figure lift is a technique which involves some dangers but at the same time it is rich in visual effects. I use it a lot in my choreography and I teach it to advanced students in Paris. Of course, one must be very careful. In my classes, even when talking about an exercise which must be done in pairs, I require the presence of a third person to lay out a mat for the couple's safety. One must be very careful not to cause accidents or injury. Having an insurance policy is essential.

In earlier Butoh groups, the figure lift was also used. But dancers just used their force without using the method consisting of progressively shifting their bodyweight. Nor did they take into account the importance of breathing and after-effects, so lots of accidents happened. A dancer I knew broke his leg and I also hurt my head because of a bad fall. I regret terribly that Butoh dancers in the 80s were so ignorant about the proper use of contact improvisation in their practice of the figure lift.

Photo: Takeshi Miyamoto
Dancers: Juju Alishina,
Jean-Gabriel Manolis
2012 Paris

The need to exchange weight without getting hurt or hurting one's partner stimulated technical developments […] dancers focused on how to control and soften the actions of falling, rolling, catching, and supporting. (Novack 1990, p.114)

~ 2.4 ~

Qi transmission, connections

In this section I will propose some new exercises linked to Qi. We have already learned in Part 2, 2.1, how to make Qi circulate throughout our body. In Part 2, 2.2, we learned how to convey the wave from person to person. In this section, we are going to analyze how to improvise while staying in contact with other dancers.

I devised most of this section starting from contact improvisation. The training I propose is very different from the method developed in the United States (see Part 2, 2.3). Contact improvisation has numerous points in common with the *Noguchi Taiso* and Qi exercises. That is why it is often integrated into Butoh techniques.

In my classes, to show students what it means to be "in contact with other dancers," I do the following demonstration with one of them.

person comes from the right, another from the left. They pass one in front of the other following parallel trajectories without crossing gazes. At this moment no contact exists between them.

Two people are on stage but it seems like there is only one.

A person comes from the right, another from the left. They cross by greeting each other. Even if there is no physical contact, mental contact is established.

Same situation: the two shake hands.

This time there is physical and mental contact.

Dancing in pairs is not simply a case of 1+1=2. If one takes into account the Qi resulting from the contact between the two people, dancing in pairs is more like 1+1=3.

After having shown the examples above to students, I ask them to work in pairs in order to do the following exercises:

Consider the Qi existing between you and your partner to be like a balloon. The most important thing is that you imagine the same thing; you have to share the same image of the object.

Exchanging a balloon full of Qi (in pairs)

- ⊃ At the beginning use a plastic balloon, for example, a beach ball, and play in order to get the feel of it.

- ⊃ Create an imaginary balloon by manipulating the Qi and throw it to your partner.

☉ First do a standard pantomime. Decide the size and weight of the balloon and practice playing in the most realistic way.

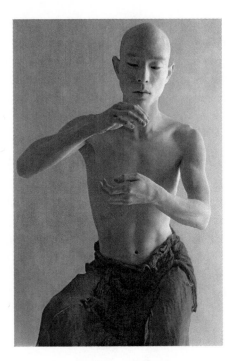

Holding a Qi balloon
Photo: E de'Pazzi
Dancer: Ippei Hosaka
2006 Paris

☉ Then deal with the balloon as if it were shrinking, getting longer, shorter, heavier and lighter. This will allow you to enlarge your range of improvisation.

☉ Starting from this balloon, imagine things such as dreams, hope, money, love, time, instead of just the balloon. Develop your imagination so that the balloon can finally represent abstract things instead of concrete ones.

Afterwards move on to the following stage: exchanging Qi with your partner. The Qi is now an abstract invisible object having no form.

At the beginning work on simple themes, then progressively increase their complexity. Sometimes students at an advanced level try to compose complex dances right at the beginning. However, if everyone dances as they please, learning together loses meaning. Exercises like these must therefore be done following all the stages described above meticulously.

Blind person and guide (in pairs)

This exercise consists of abandoning one's body to the will of others. Find a partner and decide together who will be the guide (G) and the follower (F).

G walks at a normal pace through the training room leading F by the hand. G decides everything and F just has to follow as if the body were not following his or her own will.

Exchange roles.

Once F gets used to this, he or she closes his or her eyes and G slows the pace, carefully leading F so that he or she will not hit other students, pillars or walls. If F does not trust G, he or she cannot go ahead with confidence. G has absolute responsibility. Exchange roles.

Even with eyes closed, one can discern the intensity of light in the different places in the room. Light is stronger or weaker according to one's position in the room, and F is naturally more worried in darker places. Sometimes students playing the role of F tighten their grip and grasp the hands of G.

Once one gets used to the situation, Qi can be perceived all around. One starts to feel the difference in the density of Qi: it changes according to the space surrounding a person. It is different if one is in a large space or next to a pillar, a wall or another person.

When we do this exercise in the training room, I dedicate only a few minutes to it; in summer workshops, in the open air, we practice it for half an hour (see Part 3, 3.7 *Strengthening the five senses*). Since keeping one's eyes closed for a long time is rather bothersome, we generally use a blindfold.

Training to welcome contact with other people (in pairs)

F stands up. G slightly pushes his or her shoulders, head, back and knees. F reacts to these inputs. F cannot move as he or she pleases. On the contrary, he or she must be totally attentive to the information coming from G. Exchange roles.

The wind and the tree—exchange of Qi without physical contact (in pairs)

Do the exercise above without touching your partner. G plays the wind and F a tree blowing in the wind. F therefore reacts to G's inputs.

First do this exercise by keeping your position, then changing position. Since the instruction does not consist of imitating a real tree, you can change position.

Divide students into two groups. Within each group, students form pairs. The members of the first group sit down and observe the others doing the exercise.

After several minutes, exchange roles.

By observing the others playing the wind and the tree you will notice several things. Sometimes the wind will appear sadistic, being active when the tree is passive. When the wind does not care about the tree, it plays the main role on stage and the tree becomes a mere set element. At the same time another point of view can be adopted; one can imagine different relationships: think about, for example, what would happen if the manipulator were the tree.

Transmission of Qi through Japanese fans (in pairs)

Practice the exercises above with a fan. Convey the Qi through the fans. Remember to also use the hand not holding the fan and the other body parts.

To do this exercise correctly, one must have acquired the fan dance technique and must have training fans. In fact, I only teach this technique at university or in regular classes. I never teach it in short-term workshops.

The challenge of the exercises included in this section is to abandon one's body to the stimulus received from one's partner. What is important is *not* following the master, as is usually required during training. A student who is busy imitating the master stops progressing.

The needle and thread (individual/in pairs)

Stand with a partner leaving some space between you. Hold an imaginary needle in the air and pass a thread into the eye of it. Run through a part of your body with the needle. The needle crosses your body (see Part 2, 2.2 *Waving*) and you can bring it out through any part of your body. Pierce another part and repeat this process.

The movements and postures vary according to the trajectory of the needle and thread, producing a very beautiful visual effect. What are you going to sew with this needle? After having practiced this exercise alone, do it with the person next to you, then exchange roles.

The slap (in pairs)

Sit down facing your partner. A hits the right cheek of B by touching it lightly. After having received this slap, B turns completely then comes back to the initial position like in *daruma* (a traditional Japanese children's game).

Look at the picture below.

A hits the left cheek of B, by lightly grazing it. In receiving the slap, B turns completely then comes back to the initial position.

Repeat the exercise by exchanging roles.

This exercise not only aims to have one move passively following the partner's stimuli, but this aim is also *to amplify small stimuli.*

Of course, you move using your own physical force, but you have to behave as if you were driven by your partner's.

During a football match, some players roll on the field in an exaggerated way as if they had been hit very violently when in reality they were barely touched. They do this in order to make their adversary get a yellow or red card. This movement consists of doing the same: amplifying a small stimulus.

At the beginning, you have to react to the slap with the same force your partner uses. Little by little, train by gradually amplifying the intensity by many degrees.

Arm wrestling (in pairs)

This training requires a large space.

STAGE 1

Facing your partner, lie on your stomach, lift your torso and take up an arm-wrestling position. Clasp your right hand with your partner's right hand.

A slightly pushes B. B turns towards the direction in which he or she has been pushed.

Do the same with your left hand, then exchange roles.

The one who is pushed must let go and allow this input of energy to reach the ends of his or her body.

STAGE 2

A pushes B slightly with one hand. Starting from this stimulus, this time B rolls all the way to the end of the training room and then comes back to the initial position. This exercise, similar to the one above, also aims at amplifying a small stimulus.

The human body does not have a perfect cylindrical shape, so if you do not control your body in order to make it roll horizontally, you risk going diagonally.

STAGE 3

A pushes B lightly with one hand. From this input, B turns and goes into the *seiza* position then returns to the initial position. The principle is the same as the exercises mentioned in the previous section.

STAGE 4

The same exercise as in Stage 3, but starting from a seated position.

STAGE 5

Facing your partner, start from the standing position to come back to the same position once you have rolled. The basis of this exercise is the same as the break fall in judo and aikido. These techniques are, in turn, also used in volleyball to enable players to recover as soon as possible after a fall.

ROLLING

The movement consisting of rolling endlessly on the floor has been used a great deal by Anne Teresa De Keersmaeker, a Belgian choreographer. In contemporary dance, this movement was in vogue in the 90s. The training for contact improvisation thus includes an exercise in which several dancers roll in parallel to form waves on which the "swimmers" are carried. This is an exercise that I also use in my classes.

After having rolled for a long time some nausea could occur. This is a natural phenomenon, similar to seasickness. In this case, once you have vomited and drunk some water, you will feel better right away and you can start training again.

The technique in Stage 5 (starting from a standing position you roll on the floor to come to the initial position) is actually very impressive from a visual point of view; this is why I often use it on stage. To roll, it is suggested to round one's shoulders and back. Look at the picture below.

While a ball rolls smoothly without hitting anything, a cube will not since the corners sharply hit the floor. The body cannot be completely round but if you bend it as much as possible, you will avoid having bruises all over your body and you will be more beautiful to look at.

What enables the body to stand up without using the hands after a roll is abdominal strength and flexibility in the hip joint. Basic exercises such as those in Part 1 must therefore not be neglected. At the beginning use your hands, then, little by little, try to do the same exercises without using them. Train by binding your hands with string. If, despite your efforts, you still cannot do the exercise without your hands, the *kosukumani* exercise, which will be described in Part 3, will be very useful.

Simulated fight—exchanging punches (in pairs)

This is a classic theater exercise. Fighting for real just to show this on stage is of course unthinkable. This is why actors amplify the stimulus received as if they had been bruised by blows. By rolling or kicking, performers can give an impressive show. Since the fight is choreography, they do not get hurt. Approach this exercise with complete peace of mind. Besides fighting techniques in pairs, there are also simulated fight techniques allowing several people to take part in combat.

Dodging (in pairs)

Dodging is a technique which enables one to avoid a hit in fencing or boxing. This technique is therefore fundamental for fight simulation. It allows one to train for a liveliness in gestures and movement.

In my classes, in approximately 2002, we did a lot of exercises to make gestures more energetic and to avoid strikes systematically. Since these exercises were done using a soft paddle, there was no risk of getting hurt. Nevertheless, this type of training requires extreme concentration. In addition it burns a lot of calories so it is very good for losing weight.

You must therefore keep in mind that the simulated fight training proposed in this book does not intend to promote violence but only to improve one's physical strength.

~ 2.5 ~

Standing up, walking

Standing

When talking about dancers the following expressions are often used: "his standing position is not good," or "her standing position is very strong." Where does this degree of intensity come from?

The classical Japanese dancer, Hanayagi Chiyo says that one can judge a good dancer from how they take a pose. If the natural posture of masters and good dancers is perfect, it is because it is the result of their professional and personal experience. Thus, the external form corresponds to that of the soul.

Until 1992, I used to dance by standing only rarely; most of the time on stage I used air techniques or I danced lying down. Maybe it was because, not being very tall, I was not confident enough in my standing position. Moreover I was still influenced by some prejudices. I thought that using ordinary positions

Photo: Camille Perrière
Dancer: Juju Alishina
2003 Paris

or movements was improper and that one should use only unusual ones. This is why I avoided natural actions like standing up and walking. Today, when needed, I do not hesitate to use my "uprightness," even for a long time.

Ritsuzen

Ritsuzen is a form of oriental meditation which is practiced by standing. In China, there is also a form of Qigong practiced in a standing position called *tantoko*: one stands straight as a ramrod.

In being constrained to immobility, one's brain is less distracted and one's conscience is clearer; this has a positive influence on health (see Part 3, 3.1 *Immobility*).

How to stand correctly

When I was a child, I found it very hard to stand up during the morning assemblies[1] and I felt light-headed. This was due to bad posture. At this time, in the 60s and 70s, there were no dance or physical education classes in Japan where one could learn the right way to stand. Over time, the Japanese became more exacting about ways of standing. Nevertheless, this matter always remained ambiguous (in dance class we were simply told "stand up straight!") so children could not learn how to stand properly.

You will now learn the standard method for standing correctly. Put your body against a wall pressing the back of your head, the shoulder blades, the bottom and the heels into the wall. In current Japanese body dynamics, when these four points are aligned, one is considered to be standing *correctly*. If one is not able to align these four points at the same time, it is very likely that the iliopsoas muscles are weakened, which in turn can cause stomach prolapse or gastric ptosis.

The vertical position is unique to human beings. Animals never stand for a long time. In the following section we will train by doing the movement called "the standing beast," imitating a bear standing

---

1   In Japanese primary school, once a week, there is a morning assembly where students stand in the schoolyard in rows like soldiers and listen to the school director's speech.

on its hind legs. The center of gravity of *homo sapiens'* ancestors was located further forwards than ours. With human evolution, it moved backwards.

Teach your body how to stand correctly first by standing against a wall, then by training without support. Stand in the middle of the training room. Equally distribute your weight on the legs, stretch, firm up your abdomen, lower your shoulders and let your arms fall naturally at your sides. Imagine having the sky above your head and pushing it upward. Imagine that the *tsubo* (the pressure point) in your head called *hyakue* and the ones in the middle of the soles of your feet, the *yusen*, are connected by a line and that this line goes all the way up starting from the floor.

How to stand on stage

Since performers must always play different roles on stage, they rarely adopt the posture described above. One's sex and personality must also be taken into account according to the role that one chooses to play. Thus, there are as many way to stand as there are situations. In addition, one can also try to express symbolic or abstract meanings with the body.

It is best to learn to stand "neutrally" during the course, as if starting from a blank slate. You will never progress as a performer if you always play the same roles or if you can only play yourself.

The S position

This is a position that I often use on stage. To adopt this position one must stand and look to the side, curve the torso and stretch the hips upwards putting one's weight on the back of the legs. To properly arch your back, please refer to the back exercises in Part 1, 1.2.

᧐   Stand at a 45-degree angle.

᧐   Bend your knees and lower your hips.

᧐   Keep the lower part of your body in this position and pivot the torso so that you end up looking straight in front of you.

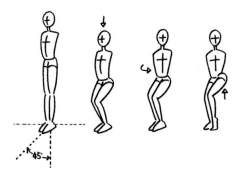

The S position allows you to form an "imaginary" body. The chest and the bottom are lifted diagonally, which is not an ordinary position. The entire body seems to be part of a wave connecting the sky and the earth. In the picture on the right, the body only corresponds to the portion indicated by the arrow, but I personally imagine it as continuing upwards and downwards.

The unreal S posture of *legong* dancers is very evocative. The pleasure of the performing arts lies in the emotions provoked by the sight of characters or things which are completely extraordinary, different from what is familiar and that can be encountered only through imagination or the creative process.

Unfortunately, the S position has a harmful influence on the vertebrae. In the Alexander technique[2], this position is considered bad posture. Look at the pictures on page 162. The one in the middle represents correct posture. Those on the sides are deformed postures. The picture on the left shows the vertebrae when one adopts the S posture.

---

2   The Alexander technique is a body educational process conceived and systematized by Frederick Matthias Alexander (1869–1955). Some students of mine teach this technique.

Nowadays, the fact that performers may sacrifice their health or their own life for art is not accepted by the public. For example, the practice of castrating young men before their voice changes, making them eunuchs, is now considered barbaric.

Anyway, magic continues on the stage. So there are means to practice amazing, "magical" art using the body while maintaining one's health. How do some people stay in good shape even after years of unnatural positions while others ruin their health in just a few months? I developed my method to answer questions like these.

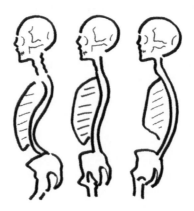

Artists performing on stage (dancers) must do exercises to maintain and improve their health. This principle has been adopted in recent years.

In my workshops, for example, I introduce notions of chiropractice and I integrate each dance class with a few hours of shiatsu, placing great importance on the care of the body. Under the direction of Toshi Ichikawa, a master of shiatsu who I regularly invite to my classes, students learn to massage each other. Shiatsu is an practice of oriental medicine which has been used widely in France for a very long time.

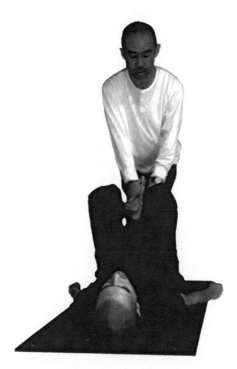

Photo: J.A/Toshi Ichikawa
and Nelson Ferreira
2008 Paris

Coming back to good posture, I make sure that in my daily life my spine is as straight as possible. In addition, after having arched my back, I rest my back in a curved position. This is also valid for the mind.

No matter the role played on stage (most of the roles are monsters, ghosts, animals or inanimate objects), I return to a normal state as soon as I leave the world of the arts. I continue practicing the exercises taught in this book regularly and without exception. In other words, each day I get back in shape both physically and mentally. The fact that I have carried out my professional career without any problems for 30 years, and that I still have the same body as before giving birth to my son, confirm the efficacy of this training.

Walking
Natural walking (group)

How do you usually walk? Walk together from one side to the other of the training room at a normal speed, as you usually do. Focus your attention on the way you usually walk so that you can remember it. What happens in your heels, knees, hips and hands?

Walk together slowing your usual rhythm as much as possible (you must take more than 3 minutes to go 15 meters (about 16.5 yards).

Running (group)

Run together from one end of the training room to the other at full speed. Focus your attention on the way you run, so that you can remember it. What happens in your heels, knees, hips and hands?

In general, feet touch the ground starting from the heel, the arms swing widely (right arm and left leg and vice versa). The knees are higher than when one walks and the step is longer. Then practice in slow motion. Reproduce the movements as precisely as you can.

This time, run as if you were chasing something. Each person imagines what they are chasing. For example, you can chase something tangible like a bird or your lover, or something abstract like an objective or an ideology. Share your impressions.

Walking in slow motion requires more ability than walking at regular speed. In slow motion it is difficult to keep your balance since it requires high concentration: if you keep your legs lifted up for a long time, you will tend to become unstable.

You will also notice that when you walk in slow motion, you do it differently. You tend to walk in *nanba* (walking without alternating one leg to one arm) or to put the foot on the ground starting from the tip.

I always ask my students to express their impressions: "A bunch of people walking slowly while staring straight ahead looks creepy and reminds me of a horror movie," or "We look like we're hypnotized."

Walking on a line

The way models walk during fashion shows is becoming more and more natural nowadays. Even though this depends on the type of fashion show and clothes to be displayed, models generally walk rapidly and take long steps, without swaying too much.

Here, we are going to practice walking in a straight line (I-shaped), as models did in the 70s.

- ☉ Imagine a line to walk on. Cross your legs one in front of the other and walk, keeping enough space between them so that they do not rub together too much, and put your heels on the ground first.

- ☉ While walking forwards, look at your feet.

- ☉ When coming back look straight in front of you. Do not walk with your legs bent; stretch them backwards, and keep your bottom up.

- ☉ Focus on keeping your thighs together so that no space is visible in the backlight. Imagine that you are walking over water while holding a sheet of paper with your thighs. Carry it with care so that it doesn't fall in the water.

- ☉ Go forwards slowly on this straight line as if you were scraping your feet on this line.

- ☉ Accompany the movement of your legs with the arms without swinging. You will obtain a more or less swaying walk, but you mustn't walk with the intention of swaying—it will come naturally as you follow the form and movements above.

There is also another way to walk on a line: one walks rapidly on tiptoes and, only after having done ten steps, does one lower one's heels.

Special walks

In my classes, students learn different ways of walking, which are only used on stage and never in everyday life. The *sotohachimonji* or *oiran* way of walking is one of these methods. Some teaching material such as a video of kabuki will help you learn and practice the stage walks.

Suriashi—*moving by sliding*

The *suriashi* is used in Noh theater, classical Japanese dance and Butoh.

BASIC POSITION—ACCORDING TO THE NOH KANZE SCHOOL

I learned this method from the master Tetsunojo Kanze (the eighth of his family) in person.

Keep straight and bend over: your hips lift up. Keeping your hips this way, come back to a standing position.

Act as if you were carrying something very heavy, move forwards without bending your knees by scraping the soles of your feet on the ground. Hips must be independent from each other as much as possible.

Put your left heel forwards as if you were pushing it forwards while sliding the sole of your foot on the floor. When the left foot goes beyond the right one, lift the tip of your left foot by three centimeters (about one inch) then put it on the floor. Move your right heel forwards while sliding your foot on the floor. Repeat these movements to go forwards.

Some classical Japanese dance schools do not lift the tips of the feet, but the heels instead, each time one foot goes past the other.

What is fundamental is carrying the shape, carrying the body by always remaining at the same level.

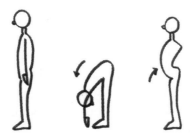

The Noh starts with the entrance of a performer from the *hashigakari*.[3] In classical Japanese dance, this is the same with the exception that dancers are already on stage when the curtains go up. What the audience sees is a performer coming in by walking. As a consequence you can see how important walking is.

In contemporary dance or theater as well, walking when entering or leaving the stage or when moving from one place to another, is very important and attracts the attention of the audience. Performers often think about the movement that they are going to make once they get to the middle of the stage, neglecting the walking required to get there. It would be nice to edit this out, as in a movie. There is only one way to achieve this result: playing with the lighting.

Among the different methods used in modern dance in the 70s and 80s, there was one in which the performers entered the stage running in order to go to their place and they left the stage in the same way after having danced, to make way for the next group of performers. This noisy race was not beautiful at all. Strangely, dancers did not focus their attention on the running. In the theater, running on stage was traditionally considered invisible. Now, it is often the opposite and this worries me, since something ugly is often more noticeable to an audience.

Sliding is more beautiful than running by lifting the legs. In addition, one can also move rapidly on stage. In ice dancing, where dancers skate at full speed, they often occupy a large space.

---

3   The *hashigakari* is a hall placed on the left of the stage of Noh (the *hon-butai*) from the point of view of the audience.

In the repertory of the *Théâtre du Soleil*,[4] there is a piece in which the actors move on the floor through pulleys. I found this device very efficient to change the setting rapidly without curtains. In addition, when pulleys are used, one can observe how actors move on stage even when this is not part of the theatrical play. We are going to keep learning the *suriashi* (moving by sliding).

In Butoh, the center of gravity is still lower than in the Noh. Bow the torso and arch the hips in order to obtain a beautiful S.

Repeat these movements several times then, keeping this position, start to walk by sliding.

Here I introduce a training method that I found efficient and that I also personally practiced in a class at Denison University in the United States.

Put a book on your head and walk without dropping it. Then put a sheet of paper between your thighs and walk without dropping it. Lastly, use the book and the paper at the same time (see picture). This exercise will enable you to greatly improve your walking.

As for the arms, open your elbows as if you were wearing a *kamishimo*[5] and put your fingers on your bones. Do not bend your wrists. Keep your neck straight without lifting your shoulders.

Model: Laura Berger,
Denison University student.

---

4   N.d.T.: *Le Théâtre du Soleil* (the Theater of the Sun) is a Parisian avant-garde stage ensemble founded by Ariane Mnouchkine, Philippe Léotard and fellow students of the *L'École Internationale de Théâtre Jacques Lecoq* in 1964 as a collective of theatre artists. The company creates new theatrical works using a process based on physical theatre and improvisation.

5   The *kamishimo* is traditional ceremonial clothing worn by Japanese samurai since the seventeenth century. The large shoulder span of the waistcoat has an original shape. The *kamishimo* is still worn during ceremonies or festivals.

What is very strange is that some students can do the *suriashi* immediately, while others cannot do it even after several years. This also happens to expert dancers. Personally speaking, I couldn't do the *suriashi* well 20 years ago, but thanks to new methods and a seven-year training period, I was able to achieve a satisfactory level. Even if this takes time, you will definitely succeed in doing the *suriashi*. All you need to do is be consistent in your practice.

In the Butoh group I was part of, the way *suriashi* was done was often criticized, but nobody offered any concrete solutions, meaning that no methods existed at that time.

This is why I created my own method.

In addition, I learned things that I would not have discovered in other ways.

Sumitori

When changing direction by 90 or 180 degrees while sliding, one does the *sumitori*.

The Japanese tend to attach importance to details. For example, if one does not fold the kimono by keeping the corners even, there will be superfluous folds. One must therefore train one's fingers starting in childhood, by practicing origami. In origami every fold must be done carefully and precisely. Even though there are some origami workshops in Paris, this is not a specialty of Europeans. It seems to me that they find it difficult to fold paper while keeping the edges even.

When cleaning one's house, the corners are as important as the rest. If you do not dust them you will be reproached like this: "you clean a square room by drawing a circle." There is also a Japanese expression "peeking in the corners of the bento box" (looking for the bug).

In Japanese, affirmations are nuanced with details. In dance as well, details such as finger movements are important.

Let us now return to our walk.

To do the *sumitori*, clasp your feet at the moment at which you get ready to change directions, then turn your external foot as if you wanted to wrap the other one.

While the external foot turns, the internal foot is still. As soon as the first has finished turning, the second changes direction by 90 degrees.

The two feet are practically touching the whole time.

In doing the *sumitori*, you move forwards by creating a square with your feet.

When you train in a group, make a row and do the exercise in turns. When the first person gets to the corner, the second starts sliding, and so on. Practice while waiting your turn. You can also relax while waiting but do not forget to observe the others in order to understand how they do the movements.

SEVERAL IMPORTANT POINTS

If your body flops around, you cannot slide with grace.

In reality you slide on a horizontal floor, but if you imagine that you are sinking into the ground, you will actually slide more gracefully. When the body becomes light, the feet tend to flap and the torso is unstable, which ends up producing an ordinary walk. In western dance, dancing with lightness is seen as something beautiful. It is the same in certain types of classical Japanese dance. Nevertheless, in the case of *suriashi*, in order to slide elegantly, you must press your feet on the ground as you do when you clean the floor with a cloth.

Some people can do the *suriashi* barefoot. Personally I cannot do it without wearing *tabi* socks (traditional Japanese socks). Traditional *tabi* with thick soles are to be preferred to nylon socks. The *tabi* with rubbery, anti-skid soles are not suitable.

The *tabi* get worn out after *suriashi* training more quickly than after other types of training. They are subject to wear and tear so be ready to throw them out after about ten uses.

Application and transformation of the sumitori

There is a way to pivot where one slightly opens the external foot and another which consists of changing directions after jumping.

Application and transformation of the suriashi

- ☉ After having slid with knees bent, stand up little by little then suddenly bend your knees again. Repeat this movement.

- ☉ Change the position of your hands. Move your hands, wrists and torso while continuing to slide. Students can freely create series of movements based on the *suriashi* after having learned the basics.

INCREASING THE SPEED

The *suriashi* shows all its beauty when it is done rapidly. A person rapidly sliding on a big stage seems like a doll moving silently or a chess piece sliding on the chess board. There is no noisy, clumsy race, only graceful movement.

In one exercise everybody forms a circle and rapidly slides in *suriashi* in the same direction. When one is still not used to the *suriashi*, one tends to run in an ordinary way. If people before you run too slowly, you can get ahead. In this exercise there are always some "stragglers." When you are tired you can rest out of the circle.

Even if this requires great effort, giving the impression that it is easy to do is very important. Once you have learned the basics, you will slide easily and elegantly.

As I mentioned at the beginning of this section, taking up the S position causes hip pain. After the exercise, lie down and relax your back.

Freestyle walking

Walking is a way of changing position. Walk freely. As soon as I pronounce the word "freely" the face of certain students lights up, above all after the *suriashi* training. One just has to decide the direction and speed; then each person moves as he or she pleases.

Move slowly from point A to point B and rapidly from point B to point C.

Do this exercise one after another: as soon as a student arrives at one of these points, the next student starts.

While waiting, observe the others.

What I am going to mention below is probably so evident that one could have forgotten it, but training depends on the following points:

ↄ   Being able to recognize one's dance skill level.

ↄ   Finding the means to improve one's technique.

ↄ   Putting these means into practice.

ↄ   Being aware of progress made.

Training means putting this process into practice. The first point requires a model, a mirror and from time to time a measurement tool.

ABOUT THE MIRROR

Usually I teach in a training room equipped with mirrors, whereas other teachers never use mirrors. In their opinion one must look at the mirror of the heart and the body rather than at a concrete object. This is true, but the mirror is a very useful way of objectively observing one's movements and improving one's posture.

Depending on the exercise, sometimes we train in a circle without having to use the mirror. There is a democratic atmosphere, without any hierarchy. The only inconvenience lies in the fact that students beside the teacher cannot see him or her and they therefore do not have a model.

If a model is needed, it is best to train in front of a mirror where teacher and students can be seen.

WHEN A MODEL IS NEEDED BUT THERE IS NO MIRROR

Legong dance teachers dance with their back towards their students in order to model for them. Since they are in the same direction as the teacher, students can easily imitate the movements of their hands and legs. However, the teacher cannot see how students dance.

In Bharatanatyam Indian dance, the teacher teaches facing the students. They can therefore see each other, but being face to face movements are inverted, like in a mirror. One must move the right arm when the teacher moves the left one, and move on the left when the teacher moves on the right. This can generate some difficulties for the teacher. These difficulties can be overcome with a mirror. Thus, the presence of a mirror is far from insignificant.

~ 2.6 ~

The baby, the beast

The fetus, the baby

If we feel nostalgic when curling up or when on all fours, is it because we have all experienced this when we were babies? Curling up is considered a typical position of Butoh dance, used to "meditate in the body."

In the workshops I organize, students learn how to reproduce the development process of a baby. First the fetus; a baby who cannot hold its head up yet; a baby who starts turning around and crawling first by putting its stomach on the floor then without; a baby who is able to sit; a baby who stands by holding on to something; then finally being able to walk upright. In this way we learn the principles of human movement.

When I gave birth to my son, it was a hard time for me since I'd just come to France and I was not yet used to the customs of this country. I found it difficult to make future plans, and, above all, I suffered from the fact that I could not dance. Despite this, through the birth of my son, I had the chance to observe closely the development process of human movement. This was a very enriching experience even from the point of view of dance.

The beast

The movement of the beast is typical in Butoh. The most important thing is not to try to imitate the beast, but to find the animal inside oneself while working on animal positions.

Do the following exercises on a thick mat or in a space provided with tatami such as a judo hall so as not to hurt your knees.

Some people feel humiliated or ashamed by walking on all fours and therefore develop a resistance to this exercise. Sometimes they even think that this position could affect human dignity. Of course I do not force people who do not want to do this exercise. However, if you are a teacher, try to persuade your students that daring to do something towards which they have developed resistance is part of the training.

THE BREATHING OF THE BEAST—BUTOH STYLE

Stay on all fours. At the beginning you can position your hands and feet however you like. The goal is to shape your body like a tent supported by four pillars.

If you do not have a mat you can use a towel. Some people believe that taking care of one's comfort means being weak. Personally, I believe that one should first avoid knee pain which would distract one's concentration.

ABOUT PAIN

Muscle pain caused by stretching decreases progressively as one trains and, in addition, this kind of pain should be considered positive. You cannot train without accepting this.

Nevertheless, pain caused by the impact of the body with the floor, for example knee pain when one walks on all fours, is negative pain. It is then better to avoid this kind of pain. As a consequence, this must not be considered a weakness.

There are several ways to do this movement on all fours.

Breathing on all fours (upwards and downwards)

This exercise is known in yoga as the cat pose, but in yoga, the breathing is the opposite to what we are going to do. Another variation of this exercise requires the fingers to be turned towards the knees.

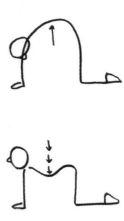

○   Breathe and arch your back like an angry cat. Put your head between your shoulders (in yoga, at this moment, one breathes out).

○   Breathe out, lower your back as much as you can, arching your back (in yoga, at this moment, one breathes in).

Once you have repeated this movement several times slowly, breathe out in one quick breath while lowering the back. Arch the back completely, then, breathing out, lower the back in three stages counting "one, two three." Do this exercise using the same method as the one described for shoulders in Part 1, 1.3.

Breathing on all fours (right and left)

- On all fours, rotate your back to the right horizontally.
- Rotate it to the left, then upwards, to the right, downwards and to the left.

The twist—the rudder

On all fours, make full rotations with various parts of the body:

- Rotate your neck.
- Rotate your shoulders.
- Rotate your back.
- Rotate your hips.
- Rotate your knees (together and touching) by lifting them up.

Repeat this spiral movement like a propeller. Do the same movement in the opposite direction.

Wave transmission

Do this exercise following the indications in Part 2, 2.2 to convey waves through the body.

☾ Imagine that a bug is crawling across your back diagonally from the right shoulder to the left hip. Then from the left hip it crawls to the right one.

☾ Imagine that a bug is crawling across your back diagonally from the right hip to the left shoulder. Then from the left shoulder to the right one.

☾ Try to make sure that the bug always moves to a place higher than the rest of the body.

☾ At the beginning you cannot do this exercise alone. Ask a partner for help: in turn, press the place where the bug is supposed to be.

☾ Repeat this exercise at different speeds.

If practiced on a daily basis, this exercise is very effective in slimming the back.

Kicking

Lift up your leg as in the picture above. There are two ways to do it:

- Using muscle strength, lift and lower the stretched leg. Keep your toes pointed (picture above, top).

- Lift and lower the right leg then hold it parallel to the floor.

Do the same exercise with your left leg. Lift the stretched leg, bend your neck and arch your back. Breathe out. Stretch your foot by pointing your toes (picture above, bottom). Curve your back and bring the leg back to your chest. Breathe out keeping your toes pointed. Repeat this exercise. Do it quickly and energetically.

Generally, the gluteus prevents the leg from lifting backwards, but if your hip joints are soft and flexible, it will contract (therefore do the exercises included in Part 1, 1.5 very thoroughly). If you practice this exercise every day, you will obtain higher hips and smaller glutei.

Flexion of the leg on all fours

While on all fours, lift your leg behind you. Keeping the thigh lifted, bend (towards the head) the part of the leg going from the knee to the tip of your foot, then straighten. Repeat this movement.

Your foot is flexed. In Japan this position is called *geta-ashi*, meaning the position with the bent ankle. Actually, when wearing the getas (traditional Japanese shoes) if one stretches one's ankles, one risks losing them. Therefore, one must always walk with bent ankles.

There are many exercises on all fours; if one does them all in a single class keeping the same position, one gets tired and cannot concentrate. As a consequence, I suggest doing these exercises on different occasions.

The beast pose
The sitting beast

The beast that we are going to perform in the following exercises is not real, but belongs to the world of the imaginary. This beast is therefore able to both sit and stand.

BREATHING OF THE SITTING BEAST

In *seiza*, open your knees, raise the tip of your foot and sit by putting your bottom on your heels. Put your arms between your knees and stretch your back to sit like a dog.

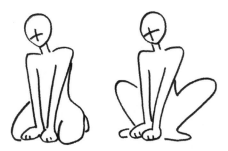

Lift your arms up off the floor keeping your elbows and fingers bent, like a dog presenting its paw.

Breathe in, lifting the right shoulder and breathe out by lowering it. When you lower your shoulder, do it as if you were pressing the right forearm on the floor, but keep it in the air.

Hit the right knee with the right hand, then lift it up and swing it downwards such as when the hawk swoops down on its prey from the sky. Breathe in when you lift your hand and breathe out when you lower it.

Do the same movements with your left hand.

THE BEAST'S LEGS

If you swing a hanging object in front of a cat, it will try to catch it with its paws. Refer to this leg movement (see Part 1, 1.7, *Hands—fingers*).

This gesture can also be seen in the *tadanobu* (fox) role in the *Yoshitsune-Senbonzakura: Yoshinoyama* (*Yoshitsune and a Thousand Cherry Trees*) kabuki play. The role of the fox or cat monster is played on stage both in classical Japanese dance and Noh. In these types of performance, animals *are seen in a completely symbolic way with stylized aesthetics, without prejudice regarding real ones*. This basic principle also corresponds to my method: what is important is not trying to imitate the beast in a realistic way, but introducing the stylized behavior of beasts into the dance.

The legs of the sitting beast

Lift your knees up alternately, keeping the leg position of the sitting beast. While keeping this position, change directions or stand up. Stretching the hip and knee joints in daily training will allow you to do these movements easily. Those who are not flexible at the hip and knee level will fall on their bottom, unable to keep their balance. Improve, therefore, little by little through training.

The standing beast

One must stand upright like a bear stands to threaten someone. One must not stand like a human being in ordinary life, or with an air of astonishment. Think about animals standing upright in a circus or when performing acrobatics.

Walking on all fours

The position

Put your hands and knees on the floor. Bend your fingers and toes slightly so that you can easily move forwards. Extend your shoulders and hips and lower your middle back. The position taken in breathing out when walking on all fours will be the normal position. Lower your head slightly and imagine that your eyes are on your forehead.

WALKING ON ALL FOURS

In walking on all fours, your right hand and left knee move at the same time (note: some animals move their fore and hind legs at the same time). Then, do the same with the left hand and the right knee. When you move your hands forward, do it so that the back of your hand scrapes the floor. Imagine a lion walking and walk proudly.

Change your walk according to the teacher's instructions. Depending on the instructions, students can become a lion walking proudly, the king of beasts or a scared dog.

A baby's crawl is different from the beast's walk. The back of the baby is flat and the movements of its arms and legs are straight. When a lion walks, its entire body undulates; the same wave that we saw in the previous section. Once you are able to do the beast movements, your facial expression changes accordingly.

The sumitori of the beast (direction change)

As in the *suriashi* exercises, to turn right at a right angle, move the right hand under the left shoulder; once the right shoulder falls softly, turn your whole body to the right. To turn to the left, do the opposite.

The pictures on page 184 show the same position seen from left, above and right. They show the person changing direction to the right.

Changing direction is spectacular when there is a beautiful mane (hair) movement. One can even see an invisible tail floating in the air.

After the change in direction, keep walking as king of the beasts.

Several beasts (group/in pairs)
The encounter between beasts

I repeat, since the animal you are playing is an imaginary one, the movement is not the same as that of a real animal.

When two animals walk in the same direction and the animal who is at the back overtakes the one ahead: the one who is ahead lowers its body and lets the other pass (first picture on page 185).

Form a circle and move forwards together in the same direction.

At the beginning, do only this exercise. Then everybody walks on all fours, each person in any direction they choose. Pass each other or overtake those you meet according to the different ways described below.

When two animals meet face to face: one lowers itself in order to let the other pass over his or her body.

When the other person is approaching from the side, let him or her go under your belly or over your back to the other side.

In another exercise, the one coming from the side rolls onto the back of the other animal, then onto his or her own back to pass under the stomach of the other.

Everybody will rest like a tired animal. Each person chooses his or her position: a cat rolled up in a ball, a stretching dog or a lion lying on its side.

Finally, ask everybody to improvise by using the techniques learned in this section (group exercise).

If you stay on all fours for a long time you will feel pain in your knees. To avoid some of this, combine the sitting beast with the standing one. If the teacher or good "animals" (from a physical and mental point of view) are in the group, they convey their vitality and quality of movement to all the others.

From time to time some food is given (e.g. a stuffed rabbit) to the group and everybody fights for it.

Dance, theater and performing arts are role-playing games. One must concentrate and walk in the character's shoes. However, a normal adult can feel ridiculous playing a beast. This feeling is understandable but it is part of the training. One must not worry too much about one's image. If one does, it means that one is not right for the performing arts.

Through this program, one can also understand if one is gifted or has some talent for Butoh.

"The strange positions that the body will never take in ordinary life confer a very exotic dimension to this practice," declare some women attending one of Juju Alishina's courses. "These postures help develop the imagination, let us unwind and go to the bitter end of our sensations. Then we feel free, light and like true owners of our bodies."[1]

---

[1]   Excerpt from an article by Jacqueline Tarliel, *Le Butô – le message. Extériorisez-vous* published in the magazine *Votre Beauté* in October 2003.

~ 2.7 ~

Quality of movement

Sometimes in a dance show, something is missing; the composition, the staging, the concept and the combinations may all be good but there is something lacking: finesse. This is due to the fact that movements do not have fundamental qualities resulting from a long learning process. Actually, effort and will alone do not help us achieve finesse: we acquire it after years of training and without even knowing it. Are there concrete ways to try to reach this result? I will give you some sample answers.

Wood, fabric and paper

Use a wooden doll, a soft piece of fabric and thick paper. These three materials will enable us to compare three ways of using our bodies.

Wood
Wooden doll

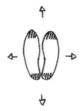

Show the doll to students so that they can feel its texture, then do
the following exercises in a group.

- Stand upright and spread your weight equally on both feet. Let
  your arms hang at your sides or cross them at chest level like
  Tutankhamun.

- Straighten up from head to toe and lean into your feet
  forwards and backwards, to the right and to the left as if you
  were exploring the entire surface of the soles of your feet.

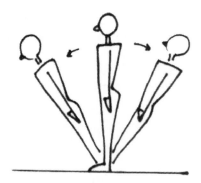

IN PAIRS

○ One of the partners straightens up and falls like a wooden doll. The other catches and supports them.

○ To start, the teacher models for students.

○ One falls forwards, backwards, to the right, to the left, by progressively increasing the degree of inclination.

If the person who falls does not feel safe, he or she will not succeed in keeping their body straight and will often put their hands on the floor. The one who is catching must therefore carefully and responsibly hold the other one up using his or her entire body.

Experiencing the two roles is very important in order to understand how to react to your partner's changes in movement. If you make sure you behave with him or her as you would like him or her to behave with you, you will make progress together.

GROUP

Form a circle of six or seven people facing the center, where one person stands. The latter simply falls in any direction and the one who is where he or she falls must catch him or her.

This exercise can be dangerous if the circle is too big. If you go to the center and you have long hair, remember to tie your hair up in order to avoid problems.

Straightening one's body like a ramrod is also very useful for the figure lift in Part 2, 2.3. The body, when tense, is light and is heavy when relaxed. You may have carried a baby and had the sensation that it became heavier when sleeping. By doing the exercise below you will understand this phenomenon very well.

○ A person lies on his or her back with his or her arms along the body. He or she flexes the body and becomes rigid. Two other people can then easily lift the person by the shoulders and legs, as if they were carrying a table or a plank.

○ Put the person on the floor.

ↄ   The person lying on the floor relaxes. This time the two people will find it very hard to lift the person from the shoulders and legs. They will only succeed if they lift the center of his or her body.

Each time I propose this activity to my students it causes several reactions: why does such a difference in perception exist while the actual bodyweight remains the same? This is very strange indeed. This principle is employed in martial arts, where we can see that when the body is relaxed one cannot be easily grounded. On the contrary, when doing the figure lift, tightening one's body will help one's partner. This principle is also adopted in dance and one should be familiar with it.

The doll choreography

A wooden doll can move due to its joints. Keeping in mind the function of the joints, progressively increase the complexity of movements. In traditional Japanese dance, the doll choreography consists of imitating the movements of the doll in the Bunraku (traditional Japanese puppet show). Originally puppeteers tried to reproduce human movements as accurately as possible, so in traditional Japanese dance these choreographies do not represent mechanical features.

Dancers seem to be handled by a puppeteer behind them. A very famous dance is *hidakagawa*, which is played with the music of *guidayu-bushi*. The wooden doll and puppet choreography is my specialty and I use it very often. Once western countries used to imitate the movement of marionettes, but today doll choreography is diversified.

All human and superfluous movements must be avoided. One must not be soft either. If you do not succeed, attach a wooden handle behind your back so that only the joints can move. Once you have memorized this sensation, you can improve your movements.

In Butoh dances some movements are similar to those in hip-hop. Robotic dance, for example, is often used in showbusiness. Dance can become art or showbusiness according to the music, choice of movements, the audience and so forth. The difference is very subtle and delicate.

Doll eyes

If your eyes retain a human appearance, the result will not be good despite all your efforts. However, keeping one's eyes open without blinking is not possible.

Doll eyes (we are talking about a doll whose lids open and close) only have three positions: open, half-open and closed.

Of course human eyes work in a much more complex way, being able to adopt a large variety of different positions. Make the effort to force yourself to use only the three positions above. This implies that all the natural movements of your eyes will be reduced to become more precise. Please refer to Part 1, 1.9 *Importance of kata (ideal form)*.

Eyes are what one first notices. Even if they take up just a little space, one can make an entire theater audience focus on this small part of the body. Eye training, therefore, is very important.

Fabric

Movement of a soft piece of fabric. One must convey vibrations through the body. This is what we learned in the chapter on waving (see Part 2, 2.1, 2.2 and 2.4).

The movement of a piece of fabric is much more subtle than that of a piece of wood. The releasing movement which is inherent to the verb "release" was frequently used in contemporary dance after the 90s.

Below, I will introduce three exercises that I did not mention in section 2.4 when talking about Qi.

For students to understand the exercise, the teacher will have to perform the following movements in front of them: unfold a soft piece of fabric, roll it into a ball and let it fall. The visual is much more powerful and detailed than the imagination; any demonstration is really effective.

Make a ball with a piece of material like a silk scarf, unfold it

(Since this exercise requires a rather large space, if there is not enough, two groups will be formed and take turns.)

- Lie on the floor. Imagine being a silk scarf lying on the floor.

- Curl up on your left side with your back slightly inclined upwards. Do this movement as if you were being pulled from the chest.

- Remember that this position represents a scarf rolled up in a ball.

- With a small burst of energy, turn to the right extending your arms and legs.

- Repeat this movement.

Using tension, release and impetus, you can move using little energy and all your body parts. It is thus a very pleasant exercise.

Floor movements are practiced on tatami or thick mats. Getting hurt to show one's will or sporting spirit is useless. One must above all avoid painful shocks to the body on the floor since this would hinder proper development of the movement.

Be careful not to twist your ankle when you stand upright on a soft mat.

ABOUT SAFETY

In France, dance teachers and school directors are legally bound to take out an insurance policy. Moreover, the teacher must ensure that students do not hurt themselves and that accidents do not occur.

Personally, each time I enter a new dance hall, I check where the emergency exit is in case of fire. If a problem should occur (earthquake, fire), my role is to bring students rapidly to safety.

Walking in the wind (with wind sound)

Walk while picturing your body as a piece of fabric facing the wind.

Do not walk voluntarily but as if you were being blown by the wind.

Sometimes, when blown by a gust, the scarf crumples up, turns or falls on the ground. Show students how a piece of fabric falls. Handle a scarf and let it fall in front of them. It will lie softly on the floor.

Since the movement above relies on a dynamic, it cannot be reproduced in slow motion and the time needed by the process to develop cannot be measured. Slow motion requires constant muscular tension, whereas imitating a scarf requires muscle release and impetus.

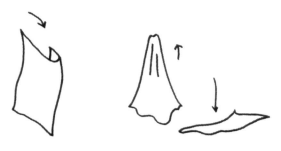

Paper

When one waves a piece of paper (as thick as a postcard), a soft waving moves through the paper from one end to the other. This is called the paper movement.

This is a movement halfway between wood and fabric. It is not as hard as wood, yet more precise than fabric. Soft, well-controlled from one end to another and often used in classical ballet, social dances and dance contests, the paper movement is regarded as an elaborate and beautiful dance.

However, if one choreographs a dance using only this kind of movement, it risks seeming banal and out of date, since the audience is used to seeing this kind of standard movement. Dancers appear to move exclusively through their will.

The deep artistic emotion in Butoh comes from what one feels when dancers' movements seem to obey someone else's will. This is why the paper movement is rather appropriate for showbusiness.

There are other examples of materials to identify with apart from wood, fabric and paper: materials like iron, plastic, gel and clay. If you can achieve the techniques described above, you can apply the movements to other textures.

Combining these three materials will be more effective than using them separately, one after another.

In my dance, *Laughing Fist* (1995), the left hand, wearing a red glove, plays a different character from the rest of the body. By dividing the body into two parts and giving different movements to each part, one can play two characters in a solo.

Exercise: combining the wood, fabric and paper movements

(refer to Part 2, 2.9)

- Training while seated—training exclusively for hands:

    - Hands embody three materials.

    - Each hand becomes a different material.

- Imagine your hand as having a different personality from the rest of your body. The part on which the hand rests changes texture.

- Stand up in order to use your legs too. For example: the knees of a wooden doll suddenly bend and its torso becomes fabric.

Improvisation using the wood, fabric and paper movements (in pairs)

One of the partners pushes the other's body. The part which has been touched becomes wood, fabric and paper. Between one material and the other, return to a neutral state.

Image training is indispensable in improving the different movements: move while imagining that your body has become wood, fabric or paper, or move remembering the teacher's or another dancer's movements. Remembering stimulates the central nervous system, which makes you choose the best combination of muscles to be used. The result is that the muscular and the bone systems cooperate well.

Image training is a very efficient technique not only in Butoh but also in other kinds of dances such as classical ballet. If you learn the wood, fabric and paper movements thinking that you will move this part of your body like this and like that, not only will you not be able to, but it will also take you too long. Instead of trying to find a solution by moving your body, have a look at a scarf softly falling down. It is likely that by practicing this exercise and imagining that you are a silk scarf, you will succeed in the blink of an eye.

However hard some people try to do the wood, fabric and paper movements, they do not succeed and produce the same result for each texture. This is due to a lack of image training or to a lack of teachers or dancers nearby, or even to the fact that their movements are too familiar and ordinary. Training must also enable you to go beyond your daily habits. Try to get progressively closer to the movements you are trying to reproduce.

~ 2.8 ~

The spiral, the 8

This section includes several exercises using the spiral and the 8. Cut a long, narrow strip of fine paper, twist it like a spiral and join the two ends: you will then have a Möbius strip. It is also the shape of DNA. You can follow this strip up and down eternally without stopping.

The 8: exercises for all parts of the body
Hand spiral

These exercises consisting of drawing an 8 with each part of the body are very useful, since these movements can be integrated into more complex choreographies. Keeping your fingers together and stretched taut is very important. If you neglect this, you will not draw the 8 with sufficient precision.

Vertical 8

Imagine wiping an imaginary window in front of you with the palm of your right hand; draw a vertical 8. Usually, the 8 is drawn from right to left, but here, since it is a physical exercise, we also do it from left to right. Repeat the same exercise with the left hand.

Horizontal 8

Imagine that you are wiping an imaginary table which is on your right with the palm of your right hand; draw a horizontal 8. Change direction. Repeat the same exercise with the left hand.

VERTICAL THREE-DIMENSIONAL MÖBIUS STRING

Imagine a three-dimensional Möbius strip with four vertical parts and three horizontal parts. Turn the palm of the right hand upwards and form a figure 8 with your hand starting from the top. At the end of the first vertical part of the 8, turn the palm upwards again on the horizontal middle line.

Then, in the second vertical part of the 8, turn the wrist in the opposite direction so that the palm will be facing upwards reaching the lower horizontal line of the 8. The top-down path is now completed. In returning, bottom-up, the palm will always be turned upwards. Repeat this movement. Do not use only the fingertips, move the entire arm starting from the shoulder blade.

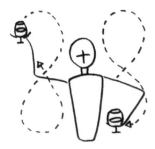

Move your hand more when going vertically rapidly, and slowly when moving horizontally, so that the centifugal force will enable you to hold an object without dropping it. This is the same principle that allows a fast car not to fall while doing a loop the loop. Practice with a glass of water, trying not to spill it (a brandy glass is the most suitable). I once choreographed a dance in which I drew spirals in the air, holding a glass in each hand containing a lighted candle. Repeat this movement with the left hand, then in the other direction.

HORIZONTAL THREE-DIMENSIONAL MÖBIUS STRIP

Draw a three-dimensional horizontal 8 in the air. Do this movement with the right and the left hand in both directions.

VERTICAL THREE-DIMENSIONAL MÖBIUS
STRIP WITH BOTH HANDS

Draw a vertical 8 in the air with both hands simultaneously. Repeat this movement in the other direction. Do this movement in two ways: (1) moving your arms only; (2) waving the entire body. This latter figure has some points in common with the movements of the butterfly stroke in swimming.

HORIZONTAL THREE-DIMENSIONAL
MÖBIUS STRIP WITH BOTH HANDS

Draw a horizontal 8 in the air with both hands. Repeat this movement in the other direction. Do this movement in two ways: (1) moving your arms only; (2) waving the entire body.

ASYNCHRONOUS MOVEMENTS

This is one of the disassociated movements included in Part 2, 2.9. At first, the right hand starts from above and draws a spiral in the air; when the right hand is down, the left starts. Afterwards, each hand advances at the same time, but at different levels. When the right hand is above, the left is below and vice versa.

If you wish, you can try a more challenging technique: the right hand starts to draw a spiral in the air. When it reaches the middle, the left hand starts the movement. The two hands start at the same time, each in a different place.

Consider the right hand as a train called A and the left hand as a train called B. When the A train arrives at the central station, the B train leaves. Since A and B go at the same speed, they move forwards together towards different points.

Do the exercise in two ways: first moving your arms only; then waving your entire body.

OCTOPUS

The movement consisting of drawing an 8 in the air with your arms is often called the octopus and it is used in choreography. However, if dancers do not respect the exact hand position, this movement will be more similar to a drowning person instead of an octopus. Generally speaking, in Japan the expression "octopus dance" means a dance with no sense or reason. To change this negative image, one just has to train.

Neck spiral

The neck is fragile. Therefore, the movements below must be done carefully, after having made some circles with the neck and after having done the stretches in Part 1, 1.2.

VERTICAL SPIRAL

Draw an 8 with your nose. Imagine there is a piece of paper in front of you: the tip of your nose is a paintbrush that you have soaked in ink. Draw an 8 as if you were practicing calligraphy. Repeat this movement in the other direction.

Draw some small and some big 8s in the air. To make the big 8, stand upright and use your whole body. When drawing the small ones, be as minimalist as possible, until your neck seems almost immobile. Imagine writing a letter on a grain of rice.

When all students in a class draw small, almost invisible 8s, the visual effect is very strange and evokes the Zen meditative state. Even if students are almost completely immobile, the 8s keep moving inside their body.

Horizontal spiral

Draw a horizontal 8 in the air, on the side. Repeat this movement in the other direction. Draw a horizontal 8 forwards and backwards. Repeat this movement in the other direction. In the same way, draw an 8 with the torso, then with the hips.

Chest

Refer to the exercises in Part 1, 1.4.

Draw an 8 in the air vertically and horizontally by moving the torso.

Do these movements in both directions.

Hips

Refer to hip movements in Part 1, 1.4.

Draw a horizontal 8 with your hips.

Repeat this movement in both directions.

APPLICATION

Start drawing an 8 with the hips; first forwards, then to the right. Draw half an 8 with the right leg. End the 8 by moving your hips forwards to the left and draw the left half of the 8 with the left leg. Keep your toes pointed. It is best for leg movements to follow hip movements, so that the legs do not move alone.

Legs

Form a line as in a classical ballet class; hold the barre or the back of a chair and draw a horizontal 8 on the floor with the tip of your foot. At first, keep your torso immobile. Point your toes. Once you get used to the movement, lift the tip of your foot and draw a horizontal and a vertical 8 in the air.

The arms and torso should accompany the movement: when the 8 opens outwards, your knee, hand and entire body completely open outwards.

When the 8 comes back to the center, your knee, hand and entire body turn inwards.

Oiran[1] *walking* (sotohatchimonji)
(see Part 3, 3.9 Kosoku Mai*)*

This is a walk consisting of shifting the weight forwards while the foot draws a lateral 8. This is called the *tayū* walk, from the name of the top courtesan in the *oiran-dochu*.[2]

Since she walks wearing the *dochu-getas* which have really thick soles (see picture above)—she can move only with the support of men beside her.

To walk, she tilts the *dochu-geta* to the side and outwards while drawing the curve of an 8 and then stops by putting down her heel.

The training is composed of different ways of walking and combining leg, hand and neck movements. The teacher will show students several ways of walking. As for the disassociated movements contained in Part 2, 2.9, one should move different parts of the body simultaneously.

Finally, all students improvise together using all the techniques acquired.

Sometimes they draw a big 8 covering the whole floor by using the *suriashi* sliding technique (see Part 2, 2.5).

The 8 techniques are very useful in dance. They are so practical that if, in the middle of an improvisation one does not know what

---

1 *Oiran*: The highest ranked courtesan district of Yoshiwara (in Edo, now Tokyo), especially famous in the seventeenth and eighteenth centuries. To help students comprehend the *oiran* I show them photos, pictures and visual documentation such as the kabuki video *Sukeroku Yukari no Edo zakura.*

2 *Oiran Dōchū:* The walking show of the top courtesan.

to do, they can be used to fill time. Knowing how to manage these techniques is highly recommended.

By the way, what is the most important element for drawing a spiral?

Well, the most important thing is to identify a central point and an axis. Without a central point the spiral does not work. When I ask my students to draw a spiral in class, I stick two pieces of tape in an X at the center of the hall. This is the departure point from which to draw their spirals. Once they get used to the exercise, they can imagine a central point without the taped X.

~ 2.9 ~

Disassociated movements

(Activation of brain functions/ training the prefrontal cortex)

The following exercises are meant to train the body and the brain to carry out movements of a different nature simultaneously. Nowadays, we live in a complex society and we often need to do several different things at once such as talking while working with our hands, walking, driving a car or listening to the radio while doing a simple task. These are things that we constantly do in our daily life. However, writing a letter while talking about another matter is much more difficult since both actions require using the intellect.

It is believed that Shôtoku Taishi (574–622 AD), prince and imperial regent of Japan, was able to listen to ten people at the same time. Even if it is impossible to reach this level, train by dealing with several projects at the same time or thinking in different languages, rapidly and with accuracy. In dance, this training is useful for complex choreography.

Opening and closing hands
DIFFERENT POSITIONS

Ɔ Stretch your arms forwards while opening the hands, refold your arms while closing the hands. Repeat this movement.

○ Open your right hand while extending your arm and close it while refolding your arm. Close the left hand while extending your arm and open it while refolding your arm. Extend your arms alternately.

○ Do the opposite movements.

DIFFERENT DIRECTIONS

○ Keep doing this movement: one hand goes forwards and backwards, the other goes upwards and downwards.

○ At first do these movements keeping the same position with the two hands, and then alternate the movement.

DIFFERENT RHYTHMS

○ While one hand goes and comes back once, the other goes and comes back twice.

○ Little by little, increase the complexity of the exercise by adopting a different position and direction for each hand.

Piano

○ Move all your fingers as if you were playing the piano.

○ Move all your fingers in front of you at chest level.

○ Spread your hands out to your sides, and then move them forwards again.

○ Hold the left hand in this position, move only the right hand to the side, then put it back in front of you.

○ Hold the right hand in this position, move only the left hand to the side, then put it back in front of you.

○ Move your hands upwards and downwards, then move them forwards again at chest level.

ↄ   Hold the left hand in this position, move only the right hand upwards, then move it back to the front.

ↄ   Hold the right hand in this position, move only the left hand upwards, then move it back to the front.

Playing the piano one cannot move the hands up and down, but here, since we are training the fingers, you can go in any direction. The hands must always move. Some people stop moving one hand while moving the other; in moving one hand, they forget to move the other. When playing the piano, one moves the right and left hand at the same time. Even if movements are very complex, generally hands obey the logic inherent to the piece performed. Of course the task becomes harder when there is no relationship between the right and the left hand.

Adding a time lag

The right hand draws an 8 starting from above. When it reaches the center, the left hand starts. Then both hands do the movement together. (See Part 2, 2.8 *The Spiral, the 8.*)

Beating different times with the hands

Since this exercise is very hard, there are always a lot of stragglers. Beat a two-beat time with the left hand and a four-beat time with the right one. Since four is a multiple of two, this exercise is rather simple. Beat a four-beat time with the left hand and a three-beat time with the right hand.

|OxxOxxOxxOxx|OxxOxxOxxOxx|

|OxxxOxxxOxxx|OxxxOxxxOxxx|

At the beginning of each measure, both hands must beat the time together.

Beating different times by standing upright

At first, one trains by beating the two-beat, three-beat and four-beat time with hands and foot at the same time. After this exercise, try to beat different times simultaneously with your hands and foot.

Beat a two-beat time with the hands while beating a three-beat time with your foot.

☺ The hands must beat the following time: O×O×O×...

☺ The foot must beat the following time: O××O××O××...

☺ Then do the opposite.

☺ Beat the three-beat time with your hands and the two-beat time with your foot.

☺ Hands: O××O××O××

☺ Foot: O×O×O×

☺ Beat the three-beat time, then the two-beat time with hands and foot together.

☺ Beat the three-beat time with your foot. Beat the two-beat time with your hands.

☺ Beat the three-beat time with your hands. Beat the two-beat time with your foot.

Master Michizo Noguchi (see Part 1, 1.4) also did these exercises during his training.

Knowing "how to"

Everybody can talk while walking, it is easy. Nevertheless, there is a difference between doing it in a place that one knows, or in one that one does not know. When one knows the place, one can get to the destination even while concentrating on a conversation. However, when you are in unfamiliar territory and finding your way around, you must concentrate on walking, since you can go the wrong way, miss a landmark or waste too much time. If you can perform one of the two actions well enough to do it automatically, then you can concentrate on the other at the same time.

By beating two different times at once, you will notice that a special rhythm comes from this combination. If you get accustomed to this rhythm and you let yourself go with it, your body will soon move along and start to beat two different times on its own with no need to use your mind. In short, there are two ways:

~ One must concentrate on one rhythm (do not think about the two rhythms at the same time).

~ One must let the body learn this rhythm (this prevents one from thinking).

Now, let's apply all these exercises to more complex choreography. The teacher will show simple examples using disassociated movements and students will imitate.

In this section, we will do two different movements at the same time using two different parts of the body. We will then integrate two simultaneous movements with different qualities into a dance (see Part 2, 2.7 *Wood, fabric and paper*). Each student will create a one-minute dance using disassociated movements and show it to the others 15 minutes later. (If anybody feels lost, he or she can use the movements included in the teacher's choreography.)

Sometimes even good dancers cannot do disassociated movements. Some people give up too soon or start to cry because they cannot do it. However, it is highly likely that even these people will succeed one day.

Sometimes I have been told that I can do these exercises because I am Japanese. The Japanese use a very complicated language in which one must manage three kinds of writing: the hiragana, the katakana and the *kanji* (Chinese ideographs). It is therefore normal that they are also gifted in disassociated movements. Well, this is not true at all. I have taught this method in Tokyo as well, and the Japanese also find it hard to do these movements and cannot always manage them.

However, thinking about it a bit more, I believe that disassociated thought is well-integrated into Japanese daily life.

From time to time, even French people change their way of speaking according to places and people. However, this *omote-ura* duality[1] is much more striking in Japan. In France, even shopowners and salespeople will often pull a face if they are in a bad mood. They are often not very pleasant to their customers. This sincerity is often considered by the Japanese to be cold and strange behavior. They first get offended, and then they end up getting used to it.

Distinction between indoors and outdoors (the inside and the outside)

In France, when one comes back home, one takes off one's coat or one's jacket, but one does not take off one's shoes and does not change clothes. In Japan, when one comes back home, one takes off one's shoes and changes into something comfortable. As a consequence, there is a big difference between indoor and outdoor clothing.

When my husband (who is French) went to Japan, he was surprised by this difference and by the fact that his father-in-law (my father) wore a suit when outdoors and a kind of pajama (*yukata*[2]) when indoors.

Besides clothing, the Japanese also use different objects and tools according to place, for example, indoors or outdoors, or the situation. In my house in France I use beautiful objects in my daily life, while in Japan my parents change the tableware, the teapot and cups according to whether the user is a member of the family or a guest. The more beautiful objects are reserved for guests.

I believe that, in France, one does not change one's manner of speech or behavior or approach towards people according to whether they are indoors or outdoors. There is little difference between the private and the outside world. In Japan, instead, when speaking about one's own world, that is to say family members or colleagues, people are very humble, and they use special polite terms for describing external people and even different terms if dealing with external people who are friends. In other words, in a family, a daughter-in-law and her

---

1   *Omote-ura* duality is an essential feature of Japanese culture. For the Japanese each being, object, organism, action and so forth has an *omote* aspect which is the public and visible face, and an *ura* aspect which is the private and sometimes negative face.

2   The *yukata* is a light summertime kimono.

mother-in-law use a specific formula of courtesy. In the Imperial family, a special formal register is used even between husband and wife.

As a consequence, I believe that the difficulty in learning Japanese lies not only in the complexity of its linguistic rules but also in the comprehension of the difference between the indoors and outdoors (the inside and the outside).

Of course, novels such as *The Strange Case of Dr. Jekyll and Mr. Hyde* show that these distinctions are not unknown to Europeans, who can understand the notion of having two personalities in a single person. But the gap between the social self and the private self is much more important in Japan.

About dance

Whether big or small, all the activities I've done in France, I've done for myself and I can talk about them openly and confidently as my own works. French dancers and choreographers usually do not suffer from identity conflicts.

But when I was in Japan, I suffered from the conflict between artistic dance (dance of the *geïjutsu* to which I aspired) and popular dance (dance of the *geino*), which was not very attractive to me but which I practiced to earn my living. This distinction was very clear: I had to distinguish between the two dances in my work.

Since the Japanese have acquired this ability thanks to their customs, they should be proud of their skill in dealing with many complicated things simultaneously. Other concepts such as the *funbetsu*[3] or the *kejime*[4] are also part of Japanese culture.

---

3   *Funbetsu*: this term means to judge well, according to reason; to be able to discern. It implies a distinction between one's self and others, which is considered only an illusion by Buddhism. By extension, it expresses an obsessive self-awareness.

4   *Kejime*: this term indicates the difference between one thing and another. It is the term for distinction, differentiation. It indicates the difference between facts and words according to moral and social rules. It also implies a sense of moderation in what one expresses and does.

Part 3

Application

Butoh class in Paris
Photo: Andrew Belser 2007

~ 3.1 ~

Immobility

As I mentioned at the beginning of this book, if one compares dance with a fabric, the weave represents time and the texture represents space.

In 3.1 and 3.2, we are going to learn the techniques related to the form and the organization of space which makes up the texture.

Immobility

To dance, one must not only know how to move, but above all, how to stay still.

Immobility exercise 1 (individual/group)

Students improvise using the entire space of the training hall. There are no indications or binding rules for speed or kata (ideal figure). However, one must dance individually, without forming a duo.

As soon as the teacher puts the music on, students begin to dance. When the music stops, they stop. The dance must break suddenly as when one stops a DVD player by pressing "pause." Students must freeze and hold their position for ten seconds after the music stops. Repeat this several times.

This exercise enables students to find a position which is both challenging to hold and aesthetically pleasing.

◯ In this exercise, the students move for 30 seconds then pause for 10 seconds, but if, for example, they move for only 2 seconds, and pause for 5, a wooden doll effect is created.

◯ Some forms of immobility are well defined, like the *mie*[1] in kabuki or the *emen* in classical Japanese dance where one freezes as if one were posing for a picture. The interest in accomplished immobility is in giving the audience the impression that time has suddenly stopped.

◯ In dance, striking a pose creates the effect of interrupting the movement for a short time. It is similar to a *mie* but less exaggerated than a *mie*.

In this exercise, one cannot decide on one's position beforehand. One must stop when the music stops. Once you have understood that a certain position produces a certain result, you can move on to the exercise in which one premeditates one's pose.

Immobility exercise 2 (individual/group)

All the dancers stay still as statues. There should be a sort of competition to see who can stay still the longest. Those who move must leave the competition and sit and observe the others. The teacher gives students five minutes to decide on the position that they are going to adopt.

Rules

◯ Work individually, without a partner.

◯ Do not lean on the walls.

◯ Do not lie on your back or stomach spreading your weight on the floor.

◯ Eyes can be moved, that is, you may blink your eyes.

---

1 In doing *mie*, a kabuki actor momentarily suspends their performance to emphasize a particularly important event or moment.

ↄ If you move or feel uncomfortable with the exercise, leave the competition on your own. You can sit or lie on the floor, but you cannot talk.

I have proposed this exercise to students from different parts of the world in two different ways:

ↄ Take a position without setting a time limit. Once each person has taken a position, start and time the competition. One by one, students who cannot bear to stay still anymore leave the competition. When only three people remain, the competition ends. Among these three people, the winner is the person who has adopted the most difficult pose.

ↄ Choose four different positions. Time, depending on the group, can vary from 30 to 60 minutes. Once positions have been decided, start and time the competition. After the first position has been adopted, one can change position three times. If one needs to change position more than three times, then one must leave the competition. The competition lasts 30 to 60 minutes.

In the first setting, one will be obliged to leave the competition if the pose is not good. Besides having the impression of having wasted one's time, one will also feel bitter. When I propose this competition the goal is not to create a race for victory, but to make students aware of their ability and endurance in staying still. Emphasizing the competition aspect is therefore not suggested. Furthermore, since it is very important for the teacher to give students opportunities to improve and progress, in recent years I have usually chosen the second setting.

However, some students prefer the first since they believe that when one has the chance to go from one pose to another, one cannot grow tired and get fed up with staying still. As a consequence the first setting puts them into an extreme situation.

In both cases the most interesting or important factor is the change in mental state.

○ At first one is strained, obsessed by the idea that one must not move. In addition one may also worry about the surrounding environment.

○ Standing still becomes more and more difficult since one's body aches and one realizes that a growing number of people are giving up.

○ After a while, one does not feel anything: neither sorrow nor difficulty; one does not care about the surroundings; one just reaches absolute peace of mind. Those who succeed are transfigured.

This is not an endurance competition, but a way to experience this state of mind.

Through dance or sport, one can reach this elevation of mind and soul "running high." I was once told that the goal of Sufi dance was to reach a mystic state rather than provide entertainment. Overall, it is believed that a repetitive movement which requires a lot of energy allows one to reach this state of mind more rapidly. Soft or slow movement is more similar to daily movements. Many dances do not enable us to reach the third stage. A "half-hearted" dance which does not allow dancers to leave the real world holds no interest. It only provokes a feeling of frustration, in both the dancers and the audience.

How to choose one's position

Another important factor lies in the choice of positions. Over time, you will discover that poses that seem easy are not necessarily so and the ones that seem hard are actually easy to hold.

In all my workshops, there is always someone who chooses the position in the picture.

In Qi gong this position is called *tantoko* (the tree pose). Stand with your legs shoulder-width apart. Bend your knees slightly. Lift your arms to chest level as if you were embracing a big tree trunk. (Refer to Part 2, 2.5 *Standing up, walking*)

In *ritsuzen* (standing meditation), it has been proven that meditating in a certain position helps maintain good health, since one can clear out everything from one's brain.

At the same time, I do not like people taking this position to win the competition. This is only a simple application of knowledge, like the resolution of an equation: "I know that I can stay still for long time if I take this position, so I'll use it." In short, one has not consulted one's body before choosing.

There is surely a pose which is specifically easy for one person and that all the others find difficult. When students discover their own pose thanks to my classes, I am really proud.

Here are some comments concerning the positions of those who succeed in standing still for the longest time:

~ Positions are symmetrical.

~ The weight is equally spread out.

~ No parts of the body are in the air: they rest on the floor or on the body.

The position shown in the picture is the one which allows one to stay still the longest: standing, arms crossed, staring forward.

However, a stable and pleasant pose is not always beautiful. For example, there are not that many sculptures that are beautiful and symmetrical. Works involving a certain harmony in dissymmetry are much more beautiful.

To study poses, it is good to refer to works of art. There are numerous dances inspired by masterpieces of western painting and sculpture. Choreography which takes inspiration from these masterpieces sometimes risks appearing banal in some ways. However, at the beginning, as for every subject, one must start from the basics and I think that teaching this kind of choreography is very useful.

One of my students, Morgane Dragon, has become independent and has founded her own group. She has created some pieces representing Rodin's sculptures by putting clay on the dancers' bodies. I believe that this training has been very useful to her.

MODEL POSE

In 2003, I was asked to choreograph poses for a French fashion magazine called *Votre Beauté*. Poses were chosen as follows: while models were having their hair styled, I suggested some poses to the photographer by showing him them and he chose some. The poses were then taught to models in the studio.

Doing this work helped me realize that poses which are much appreciated in dance are very different from the poses that a photo studio appreciates, and that photogenic poses are not nuanced or subtle. They are instead very precise: models use their bodies in an extreme way. For example, they stretch out their arms and legs completely or they retract them so that movements are very clear.

In fact all the poses chosen by the photographer were very precise and photogenic.

On the other hand, poses which are generally recognized as beautiful can be considered old-fashioned. Nowadays, shop windows and fashion magazines show models with sulky expressions or crouching down. They seem more modern than the usual models.

Since the 90s, contemporary dance communication has used out-of-focus photos or photos showing incomplete poses that in the past were considered ruined and useless. This new form of communication seems livelier and less commercial.

I took the picture on the next page during the development of a highly elaborate dance. The three French dancers were immobile. The position of the hands and the direction of the body had been established beforehand. This picture was also used for the poster of a performance in the Guimet museum in Paris.

After having been immobile for a long time, it is recommended to "wake up" the body softly, as if you were defrosting, little by little. Moving too rapidly could cause injury. A massage session soon after would be very effective. A girl, who participated in my workshop, working as a professional model for painters, confirmed that "waking up" the body after having posed for a painting was very important.

Photo: Juju Alishina
Dancers: Peggy Giraldi, Delphine Brual, Sandrine Thibaut
2002 Paris

~ 3.2 ~

Creating a picture (Dealing with space)

Picture frame (group)

In the previous section, we learned how to imagine and create a pose individually starting from immobility. In this section we are going to study how to compose a picture with several people, like a Brueghel or a Hiro Yamagata[1] painting. "Materializing impressions produced by words" corresponds to a higher level of training; this is why exercises about this topic will be introduced on another occasion.

ↄ   Start by getting used to the work without having a precise topic. Imagine that half of the room is theater seats and the other half is a stage.

ↄ   All students sit in the half with "seats." One of them enters the stage, chooses a pose and holds it.

ↄ   Another student enters and adds a pose to the first and holds it.

ↄ   All students enter the stage area and do the same, until you · have a "picture" or vignette.

---

1   Hiromitchi Yamagata (also known as Hiro Yamagata): a Japanese painter born in 1948. His preferred subjects are cities and crowds. He works mainly in the United States.

◯ The teacher provides a topic and students compose a vignette based on it. A good topic is concrete and easy to understand. For example, a pose created from the topic "forest."

A student enters the stage and stays completely still in a pose symbolizing a tree. Another student enters the stage and plays the role of a lumberjack who is cutting down the tree. Another becomes a deer. Then a hunter and a hunting dog are added. The "forest" picture is complete.

You may think that this is like a child's game, but it is not as easy as it seems. Actually if you just know the general concept of the role that you are playing without having detailed knowledge, you cannot materialize the pose. For example, when playing the role of a hunter: do you know how to prime a hunting rifle? When creating a vignette about a locomotive: do you know how every single piece works? The audience must understand immediately what you are portraying.

It is therefore very important to get into the habit of experimenting and observing your environment. Do you know how to use a fishing rod? Do you know how to knit? Do you know how to play the guitar? *There is no subject in the world which cannot be used on stage.* If you are satisfied with just body training in class, you will not be able to create complex scenes.

Concrete topics I have dealt with up to now include the following: Forest, travel, seasons, the sea, family, the city, a locomotive and war.

Forbidden topics are ones such as "stage," "performing," "dance," "picture" and "art," which have no meaning since they are implicit in the work we are doing.

The teacher provides an abstract topic and asks students to create a picture according to it. The abstract topics that I have dealt with up to now are the following: solitude, crime, love, distress, poverty and revolution. The teacher then asks students to propose a theme.

At first, one of the students proposes an abstract theme, enters the stage and creates a pose connected to the theme. Other students add to it, staying on theme and finishing the picture.

All students keep doing this work until everyone has proposed a theme. One must create a three-dimensional picture considering three different points of view: frontal, vertical and lateral.

Kan Katsura, a Butoh dancer, has conceived a program similar to mine which is called *Temple*: the image to build a Buddhist temple.

Sometimes students complain because they cannot see the complete form when they take part in the vignette. In fact, one should be able to guess or imagine the form of the picture even from the inside. There is no mirror on stage.

Those who play on stage must have "insect eyes" as well as "bird eyes" which can see from above. Having these two kinds of eyes enables the building of high-level choreography.

Moving picture—adding movement to the picture

Following the same method, one keeps building a picture, this time adding simple and easy-to-repeat movements. Following this training, you will understand that there are two ways to create a picture.

The first consists of composing a picture where every participant plays such and such a character, such as a religious scene. Another method consists of composing a picture where each person is a part of the whole (not a specific character). For example, a picture representing waves where everybody moves from left to right to simulate water movements. I was amazed by the "train" where each person becomes a part of a locomotive without having any model.

Some key points and issues with this training
LINGUISTIC PROBLEMS

The common language is usually that of the place where the workshop is being held. When the workshop is in Japan, the common language is Japanese; in France it is French; in England, the United States or other countries it is English.

When participants come from different countries, the workshop also becomes an opportunity to discover other cultures. In addition, for foreigners who learn the common language during the workshop, this automatically becomes a place of learning. The linguistic difference is actually a good thing even if it can sometimes create some inconveniences.

For example, when I organized a workshop in London, one of the participants proposed the theme "mischief," but participants coming from other countries did not understand its meaning. However, if one just uses themes that can be understood by everybody, one is obliged to use simple words and training loses most of its interest. Thus, proposing universal words which are rich in content is not that easy.

PROBLEMS WITH THEMES

Participants propose universal themes: rain, sea, wind, love or death.

When participants have different cultural and religious backgrounds in a workshop, universal topics can seem like a comfortable field, but at the same time, they risk being ordinary and uninteresting.

In general, one considers that the "theme is the most important element of a work." However, in the case of certain kinds of arts, *the body itself constitutes a theme*.

For example, let's consider kung fu movies. The point of view depends on the person: when I watch a kung fu movie, it is not because I am interested in the theme or plot. Most of the time, the theme of these movies is banal and simplistic. I watch it because I am attracted by the theatrical dynamism created by the movement of the body. One viewing is enough to know the theme and the story, but I can never get enough of seeing the admirable movements of the body.

In most cases, the movie or the dance script is insignificant. One can also say that it is a pretext to show the movements of dancers. I generally agree because *the fulcrum of dance is the body*.

Personally, I distinguish between the words "meaning" and "theme." What gives sense to dance? It is not the subject or the plot, but the details. For example, lowering one's arms can have several meanings; the movement of an arm which falls freely or the movement of an arm that one lowers to press on something have two completely different meanings. When these details are collected in choreography, they constitute the meaning of the choreography itself. As a consequence one can say that *the most important thing in dance is the meaning.* One can always place importance on the plot through cartoons or puppets but the meaning which comes from the movement can be expressed only through the living body. This is real dance. *The meaning of a dance lies in the body, not in the words describing a theme.*

THE IMPRESSION CREATED BY WORDS

In doing this exercise, one can understand the different meanings that each person gives to words. For example, when talking about the theme "dog," people's feelings differ completely.

At the end of this exercise, I always propose "Japan" as a theme. In fact, I find it very interesting to know what people think about my country, through their reactions. Almost every time, people mention the rising sun. This certainly comes from the expression Land of the Rising Sun. Sometimes participants recreate the geographical shape of Japan, each one becoming an island: Honshu, Shikoku or Hokkaido. I find this reaction much more appropriate than those of people who imitate caricatured geishas or samurais performing Harakiri (seppuku).

It is possible that those who attend my classes may assimilate my way of thinking. The teacher inevitably has a certain influence on participants.

PROBLEMS RELATED TO TEAMWORK

Through this training, students can develop their capacity to guess and participate in what the others want to do. By doing in a few seconds what is usually created after several days of discussion or experimentation, one can improve one's speed of thought.

Group improvisation allows for clear comprehension of the quality of each group; when participants are united, the result is always good, since they are collaborative and enthusiastic. Otherwise they lack dynamism and this creates lackluster results and uninteresting activities.

A scene by "*Plaisance*"
Photo: Geoffrey Benoit
Dancers: Ippei Hosaka, Morgane Dragon
2005 Paris

Those who do not use their time properly or are not on stage to observe the others cannot in turn enter the stage properly. Usually these people are the ones who find the work boring.

When I ask people to choose a theme, they sometimes propose something which is not coherent or they do not consider the others in the least. The result is that everybody is annoyed. However, when students propose a theme which is simple but not banal or overused, training becomes productive for the entire group, which gives me a lot of satisfaction.

Creating a picture for the stage

Seeing kabuki performances or operas is very helpful in creating and composing scenes and pictures. When I lived in Tokyo, I often went to the theater to see kabuki performances. Now that I live in France, I continue to study kabuki through recordings of performances.

In Paris there are two opera houses: the Opera Garnier, built in 1875 in the neo-baroque style and the Opera Bastille, built in 1989 in the contemporary style. Both are close to my home and I often take advantage of this proximity to attend the opera. When students go to Japan I strongly recommend that they go to the theater to see kabuki. Likewise, in the Japanese version of this book, I strongly recommend to Japanese readers to go to the opera when they go to Europe. In fact, the opera costs much less in France than in Japan and great operas have rich programs, are of high quality and are full of ideas and know-how regarding scenes and setting.

In "academic" genres like kabuki and opera, the scenery and setting must be very tidy as in *nishiki-e* pictures (multi-colored *ukiyo-e*) and symmetrical as in the special display of dolls on *Hinamatsuri* day (the traditional girls' day in Japan): the main character is in the middle of the stage while the other performers are considered part of the set.

In kabuki, opera and Butoh, traditional hierarchy is evident and proposes the following scheme: those who do not play a main role are meant to give value to the main characters. Especially in Butoh, the choreographer plays the main role, which is very rare in kabuki and opera. At first sight, this could seem selfish and narcissistic, but the person playing the main role has the greatest responsibility: by occupying the front of the stage, he or she is actually performing an altruistic act that cannot be accomplished by everyone. Some people will find it strange that Butoh, considered to be an avant-garde dance, is so traditional from the point of view of the setting. Well, one must know that *Butoh also contains some classical elements.*

A scene by "*Somme en bulles*"
Photo: Nazaré Milheiro
Dancers: Nelson Ferreira,
Juju Alishina, Laurent Bur
2009 Paris

In Butoh choreography and classical ballet there is not only a great difference between the solo dance and the group dance, but there is also a neat hierarchy between "a group of dancers who have worked for a long time" and "a group of dancers who have worked for no more than ten years." Between the two there are also differences in costumes, choreography and the setting. These differences are meant to emphasize the beauty of the style, which is very important, but at the same time and from a professional point of view, perceiving power relationships in choreography is not that pleasant.

On the other hand, in other contemporary dances, there are several scenes where one cannot clearly identify the presence of a leader. This is certainly more democratic since all dancers are then of the same importance. When there is no star dancer, each dancer is an equal element of the choreography. However, I find this somewhat regrettable.

In fact, the composition and the roles given to dancers reflect their position and their destiny as well as their relationships off-stage.

The content of a piece depends on each choreographer and his or her motivations. Personally I am often moved by the desire to compose a picture. Just as a movie director draws up a storyboard, I too draw up several plans in order to best decide the role of dancers, the setting and the costumes. Usually the preparation and rehearsal of a living picture takes six months.

The importance given to the visual in my work has enabled it to be included in a photographic exhibition.

A photographic exhibition dedicated to my work (1990–1996) was held at the Striped House, Museum of Fine Arts (Roppongi, Tokyo) using the entire building (four floors). This exhibition was unique since the photos taken by a number of photographers all had the same subject: Juju Alishina's body. If I could rouse the interest of these photographers, it is because of my work on picture creation. Even after this exhibition and my departure for Europe, I am still sought after by photographers and visual artists.

Since this book is primarily dedicated to physical techniques and dance, I will not add anything else on these aspects. However, in setting the stage, which is the texture of dance, there are also some important visual elements such as costumes and setting. I will deal with them in detail.

~ 3.3 ~

Sounds
(The relationship between
dance and music)

In sections 3.3 and 3.4 of this part, we will deal with techniques related to the dimension of time, which is one of the two components of the weave of dance (see *Preface*), as well as the relationship between music and dance.

It is generally believed that choreography is music accompanied by movements. In fact, in traditional dances, at the beginning there was music, then dance was added. It is also said that Isadora Duncan (1878–1927), founder of modern dance, embodied her musical impressions through dance movements. Even now, some professional choreographers create their works starting from musical notes.

With the advent of contemporary dance, body movement itself became the core of dance; music as a basis was no longer conceivable. This idea is the leitmotif of Butoh: "the body first." The dancer's body must always come before all other elements.

Among the many contributions to Butoh, there is the concept of *kikkake* (occasion or beginning), which allows dancers to dance together as a group without focusing on music. The *kikkake* highlights each focal point of dance; in English we would say "cue." In the 80s, Butoh dancers often used to yell out something like "uh" or "khoo!" as a sort of signal.

In my conversations with dancers from different Butoh companies I have often heard people say: "we received the music only the day before the performance," or "just before the performance there were changes in the music." Until now, in dance, rehearsing without music was inconceivable, but *kikkake* has become a sort of magic wand, making possible what was previously impossible.

However, sometimes the music is more complex. In this case, it is essential that the dancer who is responsible for the cues has a deep knowledge of them.

Of course the audience should not be able to guess which dancer is giving the cues or identify the hierarchy of the group. Generally, a dance becomes interesting and contemporary when this relationship is not unilateral.

Sometimes I use *kikkake*, but I choreograph dances following the music meticulously as well. I think that the musical education I was given starting in my childhood has been really useful to my work as a choreographer. I know how to read and write sheet music, I can play several instruments and I can compose or arrange music. I also have a musical ear. Even though I am not a professional musician, my gift of being able to understand, produce and harmonize sounds is a truly useful tool for dance creation.

Generally, when dancers do not progress this is not only due to a lack of physical skills, but also to a lack of sensitivity and talent for music. Dancers lacking a musical ear and sense of rhythm do not realize that they are not good. Even choreography which is easy to reproduce such as separating from one's partner at a certain musical phrase is impossible to do correctly if one does not understand the phrase itself.

However, dancers without previous musical training can be gifted and have a sense of rhythm. Dancers who have an internal clock or a sense of *ma* (a sort of rhythm) can cultivate their innate disposition for dance by embodying the music.

Exercises on sound and music
What relationship exists between past works
created by choreographers and music?

Open discussions with students based on various media (video, audio and so forth).

Improvising a dance with music (individual/group)

The teacher proposes different pieces of music. Each student improvises movements along with the others. One can base one's dance on the music or not. The teacher observes how each student reacts to music.

Analyzing musical works (group)

Everybody sits in a circle and listens to different rhythms in order to guess the time. Starting from simple times of four or eight beats, the teacher proposes asymmetric times like a five-beat time. To prevent people who do not have any musical knowledge from feeling frustrated, the teacher must create a playful environment as if one were playing a game instead of doing a test.

Improvising using kikkake (group)

Everybody, including the teacher, improvises. The teacher gives some *kikkake* to vary the movements. For example everybody joins at the first *kikkake* and separates at the second *kikkake* and so forth. The teacher does not participate in the second phase and stays off the stage (or in a corner of the room) to give the *kikkake*. When students get used to the exercise, they must give the *kikkake* themselves in turns.

The teacher asks students to reflect on the variation of the theme. For example: the four seasons, from dawn to dusk, human development, the evolution of an accident from beginning to end and so forth.

Sound production: training to improve improvisation techniques and strengthen one's reflexes (group)

One should move the designated body parts in reaction to four different sounds that I am going to list on the next page. Since this improvisation is based on reactions to external stimuli, it is like contact improvisation.

- ♩ Clapping hands—hands and arms.

- ♩ Tapping feet—feet and legs.

- ♩ The sound produced by lips "ponh!" (or the sound of a drum)—head and neck.

- ♩ The sound produced by the tongue "shah!" (or the sound of a bell)—torso.

First the teacher produces these four kinds of sounds and everybody moves accordingly. The person who produces the sound signal is called the *ji-kata* (player of traditional Japanese music); he or she is asked to reproduce clear sounds respecting well-defined intervals. Students can then move immediately without hesitation.

When students are accustomed to the exercise, the teacher charges in among them to clap his or her hands. The teacher keeps reproducing the three other sounds.

Little by little, the teacher chooses other students to be the *ji-kata*, until there are four students charged with making the four different sounds. From time to time, students alternate to play different roles.

The *ji-kata* students try to combine these four sounds and rhythms as best they can, like an orchestra.

- ♩ In order to improve the whole exercise, it is fundamental that the *tachi-kata* (traditional Japanese dancer) student exchanges role with the *ji-kata* student as well.

- ♩ Some *ji-kata* students are not attentive enough to harmony, the interval between the sounds and *tachi-kata* students. It is important to remember that managing all these elements is part of the training as well.

- ♩ When more than two sounds resonate at the same time, you need to move different parts of the body in different ways. Please refer to Part 2, 2.9, *Disassociated movements*.

- ♩ Before *tachi-kata* students get used to this type of exercise, *ji-kata* students train together so that the sounds do not overlap or play too fast.

Collaboration with musicians on stage

"Désir d'infini"
Photo: Jean-Claude Flaccomio
Violinist: Lucien Alfonso
Dancer: Juju Alishina
2010 Saint Romain en Gal

Sometimes I dance to recorded music; at other times I dance in collaboration with musicians on stage; at yet other times my dance is accompanied by musical improvisation. I have collaborated with musicians playing both western musical instruments such as the drums, the piano and bass, and Japanese instruments such as the Japanese drum, the koto (long Japanese zither), the shamisen (long-necked lute), the shakuhachi and the Noh flute. I have collaborated with contemporary musicians as well.

One can see musicians on stage with dancers in classical Japanese dance, in *Katakari* Indian dance, in *legong* Balinese dance, flamenco and so forth. On stage, musicians and dancers are visibly in harmony, which has a very strong visual effect. In most cases the choreography is strictly planned beforehand, while in contemporary dance, each dancer improvises according to his or her sensitivity.

Sometimes I take inspiration from sheet music to create a dance with musicians, but I have, more recently, rehearsed some important points such as the beginning and the end and then I added some improvisation according to the situation. When musicians and choreographers stimulate each other and nobody gets the upper hand, they can create and give a good performance. When this happens, the audience has a positive impression and everybody is satisfied.

"Somme en bulles"
Photographer: Nazaré Milheiro
Dancer: Juju Alishina
No-Kan (flute): Yuka Toyoshima
2009 Paris

"Costumes and music are an integral part of the performance and artist's inspiration. Juju Alishina, by her own admission, gives great importance to the music accompanying her dance. Of course it may seem logical for a choreographer to partly base one's work on music, but for Juju Alishina music is also a means to make atypical and audacious choices. She declares: 'I do not collaborate with other choreographers. However, I have worked with both Japanese and western musicians. For example, I have danced to the composition of a Spanish musician.' Among musicians who have inspired her dance, Juju Alishina cites with pleasure the very classical Olivier Messiaen or Frédéric Thérisod (Kaï Trio), her partner. Watching her work is a fascinating experience since, in her creations, she gives an important role to improvisation. 'I plan some movements though,' she declares. 'Alternating planned passages with improvisation is better.'"[1]

"*La main sourit*"
Photo: Makoto Horiuchi
Pianist: Frédéric Thérisod
2000 Paris

1   Françoise Diboussi, "Juju Alishina, la force de l'expression corporelle," *BITO web-magazine*, August 2006.

Relationship between Butoh instruction and sound

In some dance classes students train without music, but in my class music plays a special role. I spend lots of time and energy gathering, choosing and arranging musical pieces. This becomes the added value and the most important characteristic of my method. There are even people who attend my classes just to listen to the music that I have chosen. I have never had a workshop in which nobody asked me the titles of the works played during my classes.

Most of these musical pieces are original—they have been created by musicians exclusively for me. I find the music for my classes in Paris, Japan and abroad. Furthermore, each week, the person in my company who I have put in charge of music sends me some new pieces and I choose some of them according to the movements and exercises that I want to propose.

The sound creates the atmosphere of the place. I believe that in class we can go beyond the dimension of the everyday. Music soothes pain and distracts one from the monotony of routine. When one does stretching exercises music is meant to relax; when one does dynamic exercises, music is there to stimulate. Music develops one's sense of rhythm and distracts one from one's troubles. When doing the beast or the wind movement, music exalts the students' state of mind, making the class more exciting and animated.

In some classes no music is used. I remember that basic *Byakko-sha* Butoh training as well as the class taught by Michizo Noguchi were done in silence. Depending on the exercises, working in silence can be very efficient.

However, classes with no sound only work when the neighbors are quiet. For example, in dance schools where several classes are being held, the noise of neighboring classes can disturb students: they can certainly concentrate better on exercises through music. In this case one uses music to block out other noise. However, this use of music is not that positive. It is like putting perfume on a bad smell without trying to remove the odour. The ideal situation is to have a spirit which is strong enough to concentrate in any and every environment.

Sometimes I call upon musicians: percussionists, koto players and shamisen players.

In ballet classes there is usually a pianist and in African dance classes there is a *djembe* percussionist. Musicians can change speed, time and tone according to situations. Their presence helps me a lot. The inconvenience of recorded music is that sometimes it is no longer suitable for the content and movements of dancers. Since it is difficult to stop the sound or change music (when changing music, students cannot concentrate), students keep dancing by ignoring the music. Getting into the habit of ignoring the music is not good for educating one's ear. The presence of musicians solves this problem. In addition there is another advantage: *the energy of musicians helps liven up the class.*

OPINION OF A STUDENT ABOUT THE MUSIC IN MY CLASSES (END-OF-SEMESTER REPORT BY ANDREW PACE, STUDENT AT DENISON UNIVERSITY)

This semester I have learned a lot about Japanese dance, and Japan's culture as a whole. The Japanese are perfectionists in every way, striving to be the very best if not perfect. Years of patience and practice goes into each piece we have learned this semester. To learn what we did in such a small amount of time has given me a sense of pride and respect for the time and dedication that the Japanese put into passing down their heritage. They begin learning at a very young age and continue to enhance their skill and practice as they mature into adults taking a great sense of pride in their performance.

Through this course I was able to relax and find an inner calm within myself. One thing that I really found myself enjoying was the music Alishina-sensei selected for this course. A combination of drums, string instruments and flutes seemed to be the structure behind each song. It became noticeable to me that in order to be successful and grow as a performer at Butoh class, you really had to be outside of yourself. Willing to let yourself lose, feel the music, and let the body speak your mind.

Photo: Hiroko Itoh 2008
Dancer: Juju Alishina.
Wadaiko (drum): Mariko Kubota Sallandre.
Shamisen: Sylvain Diony.
Shakuhachi: Denys Rohfritsch

~ 3.4 ~

Voice training

Voice training is part of physical training as well. In advanced level workshops, I train participants to converse.

In musical education, one does singing exercises starting from scales played at the piano. However, since our goal is not composing or performing music, but to use the voice as a part of the body, our exercises will be limited to the high- and low-pitched registers. To do these exercises, each person must choose an easy scale: our goal is not to expand ranges.

Exercises connecting voice and movement
(see Part 1, 1.1 Breathing technique) (group)
Vocalizations (group)

Vocalize aloud for a long time as if you were projecting your voice to a wall that is ten meters away (about 11 yards).

Harmonic voices (group)

Overlap voices against a background voice. For this activity everybody sits in a circle.

Sound production (individual/group)

Work on vocalizing not only by doing singing exercises but also by producing sounds with your throat, tongue and lips.

Everybody sings a different song at the same time

At first sing by plugging your ears. Then sing without plugging your ears. If there are ten people, one will hear ten different songs, which becomes a cacophony. Through this exercise you will learn how not to get influenced by others. The teacher divides students into two groups. While one sings, the other listens.

Note: when one listens to several pieces at the same time, the most audible is the one which is sung the loudest. Moreover if one knows a song, one will find it easier to detect it. Personally I can listen to and discern the Japanese language very easily within a crowd, for example at the station, in a melding of several languages, even if it is spoken very softly. Human ears can filter information that is needed from a lot of other information. The brain selects familiar sounds and gives them priority.

Exercises associating emotions with words (individual/group)

Each person chooses a long word or a short sentence. It is best to choose a neutral word, without any emotional connotation, for example, ketchup, seahorse, a circumflex accent and so forth. Completely forget the meaning of the word and pronounce it with rage or joy. My students say that pronouncing a word like "bastard" with emotion is easy; instead it is difficult to express rage with a word which has nothing to do with this feeling. Similarly, unusual or foreign words do not have the same resonance as familiar words. Words are so strong that one can change things from black into white. So, even if in reality something is black, words can make people believe that it is white. Words have such strong power.

It is often said that "Body art does not need words." However, words necessarily overlap with the creation process and the manipulation of words is part of the training I propose.

In French a wife calls her mother-in-law *belle-mère* (beautiful mother) and her father-in-law *beau-père* (beautiful father). Parents call their daughter-in-law *belle-fille* (beautiful daughter).

From a Japanese point of view, these expressions seem beautiful in themselves.

In Japanese and English there are no expressions like these; mother-in-law, father-in-law or daughter-in-law are much colder; the "law" aspect seems to be more important than the relationship itself.

Of course, we are just talking about simple expressions, but if they do not change the nature of things, they influence our way of seeing things.

In Japan, people who work in the movies and performing arts say "smile" instead of saying "move over" or "get off the stage." This is a beautiful expression but the meaning is the same. This saying defuses all sorts of friction so that the work can proceed in a pleasant atmosphere.

Training to dialogue

Nowadays integrating dialogue into a dance is in vogue. Words have meaning and one must use them carefully. For example, the fewer words used, the more they have a certain effect on the audience. The dance piece SANGO that I created in the United States lasts one hour and there are a few minutes of dialogue. Lots of people told me that this was the most impressive part of the work. The audience tends to unconsciously give meaning to movements and to the whole work. Words seem more accessible to interpret.

Exercise to increase voice volume
(individual/group)

Read an excerpt from a newspaper so as to be heard in the most remote corner of the hall (more than 20 meters away, about 22 yards).

The volume used in daily life is not enough on stage. Your voice must be heard by the audience at the back of a theater which can hold a 1000 people. When trying to use a loud voice, one tends to scream. This should be avoided. Training is required to acquire a loud but neutral voice by using the abdominals.

Pronunciation and accents (individual/group)

In acting classes and newscaster-training programs, several methods are used to improve pronunciation. One reads sentences by clearly pronouncing each word. In Japan I practiced some methods such as the *Amenbo no uta* or *Uirouuri* when I was about 20 and was studying theater.

For example, one exercise is to read the following sentence as fast as possible (which corresponds very well to the topic of this book): *Odori odorunara odori no dori o naratte odori no doridorini odori o odore*—if you dance, dance after having grasped the sense of the dance and following this sense. After pronunciation exercises, study the modulation of dialogues as well and ways to associate dialogues with movements.

Diction (group)

Our daily life is full of different kinds of noise. While walking in the street we hear people's voices, announcements and the noise of cars and trains all at the same time.

We are now going to create music that is the synthesis of noises produced at the same time which have no relationship between them.

PROCEDURE

Eight to 15 people sit in a circle. If there are too many participants, the waiting time is too long. If there are too few, one rapidly runs out of ideas.

Produce a sound in turns. The sounds must not have any relationship to each other and they must not overlap. When the sixth person starts, the first stops. When the seventh person starts, the second stops and so on. In sum, you should hear the sound produced by five people at the same time. Everyone should know when to stop.

THE NATURE OF SOUNDS

- ◯ All the noise that we can produce by using the body such as clapping our hands and tapping our feet.

- ◯ Screams.

- ◯ Songs (existing or invented).

- ◯ Chattering (about simple things but using a rapid rhythm like a rapper). In producing this kind of sound, one can use the group's common language or one's own native language. Speaking spontaneously and fluently is not easy since the mind needs more time than the lips to express a concept. This is why I really admire rappers who are able to improvise while performing: they must have very agile minds.

- ◯ Whistling.

- ◯ Reply or short speech (part of a famous theatrical dialogue or a politician's speech).

- ◯ Dialogue (a mother scolding her children, words between two lovers or polite exchanges and so forth).

- ◯ Announcements (phone messages, airport announcements, etc.), for example, "The number you have dialed is currently unavailable. Please hang up and try again. Thank you."

- ◯ TV commercials, e.g. KitKat or chewing-gum.

We do not always memorize sentences heard on a daily basis. Even among actors, some can memorize very fast, others take more time. When I was young I learned so fast that I could recite all the dialogue soon after having heard it at the theater or cinema. However, I also have to take care since, with age, one's memory decreases and one's mind loses vitality.

An actor who develops several projects at the same time must accumulate several roles so it is doubly difficult: he or she must memorize lines as well as change of register. This is where the ability to disassociate comes into play (see Part 2, 2.9).

~ 3.5 ~

Transmission games

Usually imitation and mimicry processes are used to train actors but they are also efficient for dance training and to enlarge one's range of expression, avoiding repetition and routine.

Imitation exercises (in pairs)

Work in pairs. One moves and the other imitates. Exchange roles. Simultaneous imitation, consisting of reproducing the other's movements instantaneously, gives the impression of unity as in group dance. It can seem that those who are improvising and those who are imitating are moving almost at the same time. This technique was created in the 1920s.

TWO EXERCISES

In the first exercise, two partners stand in front of a mirror and move in the same direction: for example, when one lifts the right hand, the other does the same.

In the second exercise the two partners stand one in front of the other, as if in front of a mirror. For example, when one lifts the right hand, the other lifts the left hand.

I saw a performance at the *Cirque d'Hiver* in Paris in which the two actors, who were physically similar and wore the same costume, played a mirror using the simultaneous imitation technique.

First, imitate the movements of your partner as precisely and meticulously as possible. Then increase the level of difficulty, going from the imitation of an environment to the imitation of an idea.

THE AUDIENCE'S POINT OF VIEW

☉ At first one can discern the person who is imitating the other, but as soon as the common spirit rises, the time lag almost disappears and the dance develops fluidly. It is then difficult to identify who is imitating whom.

☉ When the two partners differ in technique and experience, sometimes one of the two cannot follow the other.

☉ When the two have a common technique (e.g. they have trained in the same repertory with the same teacher), they can give the impression of mastery. However, their dance tends to involve no surprises.

THE IMITATOR'S POINT OF VIEW

☉ In following the other's habits, one uses muscles that one usually does not use and often develops muscle ache all over one's body.

☉ Imitating the movements of beginners is very difficult; it is the same for clumsy dancers who can't coordinate their movements or those dancers who do not know what to do.

☉ Sometimes, after having been imitated, one is surprised by one's own habits of which one becomes aware for the first time.

Let us not forget that in the art of body movement, the imitator must be more skilled than the imitated. The latter must simply follow his or her instinct, while the other must be able to analyze and reproduce. This is why imitation training is used in several disciplines.

Transmission game 1 (group)

We apply the transmission or "telephone" game used in linguistic training to dance. Participants transmit a piece of information from mouth to ear. Little by little, the content of the message changes and, at the end, it becomes completely different from the original message.

Development

⊃   Students form two rows; the A row (left) and the B row (right); the space between the two rows (the stage) must be clear for movement.

⊃   People in row A stand with their backs to the stage, while people in row B stand facing the stage.

⊃   At the beginning everybody in row A sits.

⊃   Student no. 1 leaves the row, performs a simple movement and shows it to student no. 2. Then he or she sits in row B.

⊃   Student no. 2 reproduces this movement, shows it to student no. 3 and sits in row B.

- Student no. 3 reproduces this movement, shows it to student no. 4 and sits in row B.

- When the last student performs, all the others are in row B. Student no. 1 shows everyone the original movement and this is compared with the one performed by the last student.

- Then student no. 2 invents a movement and shows it to student no. 3 and so on, as before. The game continues until every student has shown his or her own movement.

NOTES

- If there are too few students, this game is less interesting since there is little difference between the first and the last movement. But when there are too many participants, people lose concentration since the waiting time is too long. The ideal number of people is about 12.

- When the original movement is not clear, its transmission becomes very difficult. One can do any movement at all as long as it is reproducible by the person who created it. Occasionally students move without thinking about what they are doing. In this case, they cannot reproduce their own movement at the end.

- When doing this activity, it is important to convey as meticulously as possible to the other what one has seen. For example, one must be able to reproduce stumbling and swaying exactly like the original. One must convey speed and rhythm as well.

- In doing this exercise, little by little one tends to add one's own habits of movement. Furthermore, since one tends to omit what one cannot understand or what is too difficult to reproduce, the movement tends to become shorter.

- It is fun to witness the joy and amusement and imagine what people waiting in row A (who cannot see the stage) feel.

- ◯ *When details have a strong impact, the essential message tends to be missed.*

- ◯ When the movement is imitated and conveyed by several people, it differs from the original one. However, soon after, it could become similar to the original.

- ◯ For this reason one might think that students imitating the other's movement do not imitate the movement as it is shown, but they reproduce the movement by unconsciously imagining it as another original movement.

- ◯ In general, the quality of a product tends to decrease through reproduction, like with photocopies and cassette tapes. However, sometimes quality is enhanced. For example, sometimes the reproduction of a commercial product by a certain enterprise is better in quality and price than the original product. As a consequence, one might wonder: has the quality of Butoh improved or become worse?

Transmission game 2 (group)

In this game each person transmits the movement by shaping it as they please, by adding or removing something. The more the game advances, the more refined the movement becomes. Transmission game no. 2 is more creative than game no. 1 and students have more fun.

Objectives and effectiveness of these exercises:

- ◯ Controlling or organizing one's own movement.

- ◯ Strengthening the memory.

- ◯ Receiving and transmitting information exactly.

- ◯ Performing in front of an audience.

On the other hand, systematizing the processes to reproduce and transmit is consistent with the desire to create a training method such as mine. One can compare this with the advantages of systematizing and creating methods in cookbooks as I mentioned at the beginning of this book. For a long time it has been said that the performing arts and dance were made of "flesh and blood" and that the only way to enjoy these arts was to witness a performance at a specific place and time. However, in this case, the number of people who can enjoy this pleasurable experience is obviously limited. However, even the art of cooking, which is very concrete, has overcome this obstacle: the key to making a certain kind of cuisine or dish is the recipe. The underlying spirit leading to the publication of a recipe or a method to promote a certain kind of cuisine lies in an intention of generosity, as if one were sharing a cache of gold with many people.

Systematization or creating methods is not easy: the more one improves one's technique and manages the art, the more difficult it is to systematize one's body movements. To continue the comparison with cooking, one cannot obtain the same flavors as a famous chef simply by following the recipe: even if the nature and quality of ingredients, the seasoning and the oven temperature are meticulously respected, there are still subtle techniques which are absolutely impossible to imitate. *When you become aware of this, you are at your second point of departure*. Until you have achieved this level, which constitutes the hidden sense of the mysteries of an art, you need a guide. This book is useful for that purpose.

In the following section I will deal with elements related to transmitting and reproducing movements on the basis of the exercises in this section.

~ 3.6 ~

About reproduction and imitation

Dance is a living art; therefore dance creations are ephemeral. We can only perform once an evening and only for people who are there. The time and space in which dance develops are limited; this is a factor preventing the popularization of dance.

When one thinks of dance as a business, this implies various difficulties. First of all, since dance is a living art. This means that the costs of producing a performance are naturally high. For example, if dancers have to follow an unreasonable schedule on tour, they cannot dance in their best physical condition, so the quality of the performance might suffer. A schedule in which dancers must prepare and perform just after their arrival in a country (without considering possible jet lag) can only be planned from a theoretical or temporal point of view, but it is completely impossible from a physical point of view. Even if one tries one's best, the quality of the performance on stage (which is the most important thing) is inevitably affected. However, if one takes into account the physical condition of the dancers (age included), weather conditions, fees and the time needed to study and create a dance, the production costs and fees become extremely expensive. When a product is too expensive, it is difficult to sell and does not yield anything.

Since dance production is currently very expensive, one just barely makes ends meet thanks only to ticket sales. Creating choreography in most cases means that the organizers buy a show from the dance company, or sign a co-production or a performance agreement. The producer is in charge of all fees as well as for the recruitment of employees. In France, the company pays very expensive social-security costs to hire dancers. Previously, the state was renowned for its grants to artists and its policy of safeguarding their lives and activities. However, in recent years, the budget for these types of subsidies has progressively decreased. Communication is sometimes overseen by organizers, at other times by the company. The revenue from the sale of the performance is either transferred to the theater or kept by the company. In most cases, earning anything without external financing (sponsorships or grants) is very difficult.

Some people think that artistic creation and business are two different things. However, if one wants to be a professional dancer, one must succeed artistically *and* financially. If the management of a company is ineffective, it will cause a lot of problems for the employees, family and collaborators. As a consequence, the idea that an artist must be ready to live in poverty seems irresponsible to me.

The repertory system is a solution which enables works of dance that are not that suitable for the market to be more profitable. In Butoh the most important thing is the dancer, much more than the dance itself. In the repertory system the most important factor is the dance, not the dancers. When a dance does not depend on specific dancers so that they are interchangeable, it becomes more profitable since recovery is possible.

With the concept of "the body first" Butoh goes completely against the tide of the repertory system. One reason why Butoh has inspired a lot of interest all over the world lies in the concept of a body which is privileged and irreplaceable. Butoh said no to the culture of reproduction which was widespread at the time. The body speaks just by standing there. This is a *no* to mass industrial production, capitalist society—the assembly line concept which neglects the human body, formal society based on career advancement and business, functionality, convenience and so on.

The concept of Butoh created by Tatsumi Hijikata is far from the world of business and of worrying about success or failure. It is a theory which focuses one's attention on details that do not conform to the rules. The value of Butoh at that time lay in the unique personality of the art produced by each single body and not in the possibility of creating a series, which would vulgarize Butoh.

Personally, in light of my experience, I have reached the conclusion that the concept of the priority of the body with its irreplaceable features is not the only factor which constitutes true Butoh. Renouncing all marketing and thinking only about the "body which talks through its own presence" limits the potential of Butoh.

First of all, body supremacy is not the principle of choreography. I think that the idea of creating dances which alleviate body imperfections is more interesting since the limits of a dance go beyond the confines of the body.

Secondly, I do not think that it is necessary to stick to the idea that Butoh is not reproducible.

In *The Work of Art in the Age of Mechanical Reproduction*, Walter Benjamin[1] talks about the new possibilities offered by the reproducibility of works of art; he says that while the ritual value of art has progressively faded and has been replaced by the concept of exhibition (in this way art loses its authenticity), a big playground appeared which allowed a more independent and open form of art.

His theory, which gives positive value to reproduction, is much more constructive than the trend of complaining about human alienation due to the introduction of mechanical work. The diffusion of images in great quantities through means such as photography or cinema offers new possibilities. *Even in the field of dance, reproduction can be considered positive.*

At a historical level, sometimes the success of a dance style leads to the birth of imitators, which in turn give birth to a movement.

---

1   Walter Benjamin (1892–1940): German art critic. He wrote *The Work of Art in the Age of Mechanical Reproduction* after having taken refuge in France.

Examples include Isadora Duncan, Mata Hari or Okuni (Izumo no Okuni—founder of the kabuki theater).

Imitators allow dance (which is usually difficult to spread) to become a movement. If one dances 100 times, the number of spectators will be limited to those who were present at the performance. However, if 100 dancers including imitators dance 100 times, the number of spectators increases accordingly.

In any case, the presence of imitators does not affect the value of the creator. After all, those who see the imitator's performance usually want to see the original.

Let's take fine arts as an example. The Louvre is not far from my home. Visitors come from all over the world to see the original version of the *Mona Lisa* and the *Venus de Milo*. One can see the reproductions of these works everywhere in the world, and yet people come to Paris to see the originals.

Reproduction enhances the effect of publicity; *the distribution of copies raises the value of the original*. The artist who created the work should therefore thank his or her imitators for contributing to their diffusion.

We can say that the key to success for a choreographer is to have a reproducible style. Of course his or her style *must be worth the effort of being imitated*. The value of Benjamin lies in the fact that he had already considered art reproduction as a positive phenomenon; at that time he had already seen a reality of today.

~ 3.7 ~

Strengthening the five senses

In this section you will find the exercises that I suggest in my summer or intensive training workshops. These exercises cannot be done in regular classes since they require a lot of time or materials, or simply because they are meant to be done outdoors.

The path of sensitivity

The path which leads to the sharpening of sensitivity required by Butoh is full of obstacles; we are dealing with a kind of extreme sensitivity which is not used in ordinary life. People who are bound by social prejudice or who are not as sensitive would have to train more than others.

I introduce here one of the most effective exercises to strengthen the five senses. Before doing this exercise, you should have already performed the *Blind person and guide* exercise (Part 2, 2.4).

Blind walking outdoors (in pairs)

To do this exercise wear comfortable clothes (to allow for freedom of movement) and sneakers (doing this exercise barefoot is dangerous), a hat or sunglasses, if needed, a small waist bag and a clock or stopwatch. Keeping your eyes closed is not easy, so the teacher has to provide a sufficient number of blindfolds. Besides, wearing a blindfold allows the blind person to be protected from danger since he or she will draw the attention of the surrounding people.

I use an elastic ribbon: a scarf does not stretch and it is more complicated to tie and untie.

I found a great quantity of dark blue ribbons in a hardware store in Fabourg Saint-Denis in the tenth arrondissement (district) of Paris. I negotiated with the owner and got 30 ribbons for the price of 25, a suggestion that he accepted with pleasure. While he was packing the ribbons he asked me what they were for. When I answered, he looked at me suspiciously...

- Work in pairs. Appoint one guide (G) and one follower (F).

- G walks on mountain trails leading F by the hand, who is blindfolded. G decides the direction and the speed. F just follows G and does not move at his or her own initiative.

- G is completely responsible for F and must behave as if F were blind.

- G must pay attention to steps, hills and slopes, cliffs or cars and avoid big rocks or puddles.

- Talking is forbidden so that F can concentrate on the input and information that he or she is receiving from the external world.

- However, this does not mean that one cannot talk at all. G gives F the information needed: how many steps there are, a car is coming and so forth.

- G memorizes the itinerary and takes notes of some points of reference.

- From time to time, when in a safe place, G can let go of F's hand and let F walk freely. However, even in this situation, G must carefully watch over F and be able to take F's hand immediately if needed.

☽ Every 30 minutes, G and F exchange roles.

☽ G teaches the itinerary to F and gives F the notes on the points of reference. After 30 minutes of walking, one will be fairly far from the departure point. One may not know the way back.

Considering the return

When I lived in Japan I often used to go jogging. In Tokyo, I followed the path going from Shibuya to the Harajuku station through the cemetery of Aoyama and Omotesando. When I was well-trained I was able to go very far; I have even experienced exhausting all my strength and having to return home in a taxi.

On a regional tour, I used to jog along a railway track and sometimes I was so tired that on the way back I took the train.

If you know your limits, you can do a half-tour to a place from which it is easy to return. In this way, you will not need to use public transportation.

If you are a teacher, make sure that the personal effects left by your students are in a safe place. I usually leave them in a locked room.

After having done this activity for about an hour, students take a break of about 15 minutes; they then share their experience around a table.

Examples:

☽ "G led me to a field and let go of my hand. I ran and felt like I was flying."

☽ "While walking, I thought I heard the sound of water. In fact I was close to a river. G took my hand and dipped it into the water; I was surprised by the cold."

Stimulation when visual perception is limited

Sounds

~ The sound produced by our own steps or those of someone who is beside us on a stony path.

~ The sound produced by our own breathing or of someone beside us.

~ The sound of trees and grass in the wind.

~ Birds chirping.

~ The sound of mosquitoes or flies and the croaking of frogs.

~ The mooing of cows and the neighing of horses.

~ The gurgling of water.

~ The sound of a car approaching.

~ The sound of a plane or a helicopter.

~ Echoes (e.g. in a church, etc.).

Smells

~ The smell of our body or of someone beside us; the smell of hair gel or styling mousse.

~ The smell of earth and grass.

~ The smell of wet stones when entering a cave.

~ The smell of chlorine when passing near a swimming pool.

~ The smell of a river.

Tactile sensation and others

~ Different tactile sensations through shoes: stony paths compared to paved or asphalt streets.

~ Water and leaves (from time to time, G makes F touch things by taking his or her hand).

~ Dust or dirt.

~ Temperature changes: a cold sensation on entering buildings like churches or stone buildings; a hot sensation in the sun; a cool sensation in the shade.

~ Pressure on one's legs and lumbar region when climbing a hill.

Once you get used to this exercise, you can feel the Qi rising around you. For example, a person will put up their hands protectively when approaching a wall even if the person is blindfolded. He or she will start to perceive their surroundings.

Students say that this work is an excellent experience: "I went to the same mountain yesterday but I couldn't perceive smells and sounds in the same subtle way."

I organized this activity in 2008 on the campus of the Juniata College in Pennsylvania during an intensive workshop. There was a forest near the university as well as elements which were specific to the campus and that did not exist in the mountains. G could guide F around the library, the cafeteria or the swimming pool.

Since 2009, each summer I have held a workshop in the center of Paris. On such occasions, we go out onto the street. Since there is real danger due to the traffic, G must be very attentive and be more responsible than ever. Students walk in the street or along the Seine, they go to the market, to the church and to the bakery. The difference from the mountain trails is that, in the city, there is contact with people. Students have reported that passers-by or owners of shops were very cooperative and that some people even said they wanted to play the game.

I tested and developed this method by myself, but some American choreographers suggest a similar activity. One of the participants at the workshop that I organized in the United States said: "I've done similar work, but I never achieved such sharp perception." Another student wrote on his report: "*The blind partner exercises were eye opening.*"

This is a way of saying that this exercise awakened his conscience. The initial objective is to strengthen the five senses. However, since this work cannot be done without absolute trust in one's partner, it is also useful to improve human and social relationships in people who tend to withdraw into themselves or who do not have good relationships with others.

In addition to the exercise above, there are other exercises aiming at strengthening the five senses. During intensive workshops, I organize discussions on the topic of the memory of the five senses, around a table or beneath a tree. Participants classify their most important memories according to the five senses (sight, smell, hearing, taste and touch). They draw up a classification of the best and the worst and tell this to the others.

Since 2010, I have been writing a series of essays under the title *The Memory of the Five Senses* in a Japanese magazine called *Talking Heads Sosho*.

It is very enjoyable to talk to people who have different opinions. One learns a lot of interesting things, sometimes unique notions, and this stimulates exchange between participants. This is an occasion to learn how to introduce oneself to people as well: put one's ideas in order and talk so that a certain interest can be created.

I had this kind of discussion with theater students and professional actors. When they talk in public, they combine gestures and expressions and know how to modulate their voice. One feels as though one were watching a show. Dancers are generally not trained for this and their ways of expressing themselves are sometimes primitive: "I would like to learn the dance instead of talking," or "I would like to move more." I find this a bit regrettable because I think that if dancers worked more with actors, they could enrich their expressive abilities. This is an evolution that I find very desirable.

~ 3.8 ~

Developing the sense of time and space

These exercises aiming at developing one's sense of space and time are also done blindfolded. They require a lot of space: a hall of 120–150 square meters (about 143 to 179 square yards) for six people and a hall of more than 200 square meters (about 239 square yards) for only ten people. A rectangular space is better than a square one or a room with irregular contours. The floor must be flat and uniform; these exercises cannot be done outdoors.

This is a simple exercise but it still requires perseverance and patience. Some participants, who came to this workshop just for amusement, left immediately. Even if it is difficult, this work allows one to grasp the sense of the body and to master the body deeply in a very efficient way.

Developing the sense of space (in pairs)
This time, the relationship between G (the guide) and F (the follower) in not the same as before: this time one partner helps the other.

Short walk of a blind person (in pairs)
Several people walk blindfolded for about five to eight meters (about 5.5 to 8.5 yards) in parallel. The exercise consists of walking

straight up till the end. Use a rectangular hall and walk the width of it.

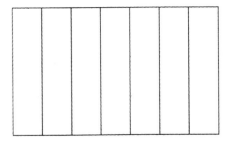

○   Walk—at normal speed, then rapidly, then slowly.

○   Move backwards—at normal speed, then rapidly, then slowly.

○   The partner who is not blindfolded makes sure that the other person does not hurt him- or herself against a wall or bump into other students. After this exercise, he or she tells the other what he or she has observed during the exercise.

○   Example of comments: "He walked straight for three meters (about 3.28 yards) but afterwards he began to go right and finally he was much more to the right than expected."

Do you think you can walk straight when blindfolded? Almost nobody can. Could it be because of the angle of the vertebrae or the way one is used to walking?

Look at your shoes: is one much more worn out than the other? Despite this, why can we walk straight with our eyes open? The answer is simple: when we open our eyes, the optic nerves send signals to each part of the body which automatically react. After this exercise, think about a possible solution with your partner and practice trying to go straight without using any input from the optic nerves. This training is useful for exercises concerning each part of the body as well.

Continue the exercise exchanging roles.

Long walk of a blind person (in pairs)

For those who succeeded in going straight for a short distance, let's increase the difficulty of the exercise. This time several people walk blindfolded in parallel for a distance of 12–15 meters (about 13 to 16 yards), trying to go straight. The full length of the hall must be used.

- ⊃ Walk—at normal speed, then rapidly, then slowly.

- ⊃ Move backwards—at normal speed, then rapidly, then slowly.

- ⊃ The partner who is not blindfolded helps the other person, as in the previous exercise.

Some students say that after having decided to achieve the goal and keeping it in mind, they can walk straight without any deviation.

Developing the sense of time
The dance of a blind person (individual/group)

1) All participants improvise together for three minutes with their eyes open.

- ⊃ At a normal speed

- ⊃ Rapidly

- ⊃ Extremely slowly

⊃   Teach your body this three-minute lapse of time. The teacher clearly indicates the beginning and the end of the exercise using a chronometer (30 seconds before the end, the teacher indicates to students that time is running out).

2) Form pairs. The first pair improvises a dance blindfolded at a normal speed. When each of the two people forming the pair thinks that three minutes have passed, he or she takes off his or her blindfold and goes to the corner of the hall. His or her partner measures exactly how much time the other has danced and notes it.

Notes: Even when blindfolded, you can still sense when people around you stop dancing. You must not be influenced by this. You must trust in your own sense of time.

Once everybody has stopped, your partner will tell you how many minutes and seconds (remember to specify the seconds as well) you danced for.

⊃   The second pair of students improvises at a normal speed.

⊃   The first pair improvises at a rapid speed (the movement does not necessarily have to be the same as before).

⊃   The second pair improvises at a rapid speed.

⊃   The first pair improvises at a slow speed.

⊃   The second pair improvises at a slow speed.

Generally, the quicker one moves, the slower time goes by according to one's perception. You will think "Is three minutes that long?"

Some dancers improvise without the slightest sound. How can they be aware of time knowing that the performance time is planned beforehand? *They undoubtedly have an internal body clock.*

What does "normal speed" mean? Generally we have the feeling that a normal speed corresponds to a resting heartbeat or to the speed of the second hand.

We perceive time as rapid at more than 120 beats per minute ($\bullet$=120). We perceive time as slow at less than 100 beats per minute ($\bullet$=100).

Dancing extremely slowly in my class means that we move at a speed of ten centimeters (about four inches) per minute: it is almost like being immobile.

One does not necessarily have to repeat the same movements as before; the important thing is to respect the designated speed.

We have already done an exercise consisting of changing speed while doing the same movement (Part 2, 2.5, *Standing up, walking*). Here, we apply this exercise to choreography.

Changing the speed while doing the same choreography (individual)

- First of all, the teacher does a simple series of movements in eight beats and all students do the same.

- Students do three versions: normal speed, rapid speed and slow speed. The teacher counts the time out loud.

- The teacher gives ten to 15 minutes to students and each one composes a series of movements based on an eight-beat time. The teacher must draw students' attention to the fact that complexity impedes speed.

- The teacher beats the time by clapping. I use a small tambourine. One can also use a metronome. During this exercise, sometimes a percussionist plays.

- Occasionally I give one of my students the task of beating time to concentrate better on observing movements. In fact, beating time is more difficult than you may think, in particular for the slow speed: if you do not count between one time and another you might not beat at regular intervals.

꘎ Depending on the choreography, there are very fast movements in Butoh and classical Japanese dance as well, despite the common preconception that Butoh is very slow. Slower movements require more muscular energy than one might think. You can not use a run-up sudden burst of energy as you could with smaller movements. It is therefore much more difficult than one might suppose.

꘎ When students improvise they tend always to repeat the same movements. The same happens to the teacher.

꘎ It would be ideal to plan regular goals, for example, creating a new series of movement each week. This will help avoid always repeating the same movements. This exercise is very useful for this purpose.

What is boredom?

In general, people think that slow movements are boring. What do you think? When watching a performance, at which moment do you start feeling bored?

Performances that I personally found boring were by one of the European groups influenced by Butoh. During the performance, one after another, the spectators left. They said: "The movements and rhythm are so slow that it's like nothing is happening," or "watching shows like this is a waste of time." I also found these performances boring and tiresome, but I watched them until the end hoping for a change. In the end, no evolution occurred. Afterwards, I reflected on the reasons why I was bored and I wondered: *what is boredom, really?*

Consider static works such as paintings or sculptures: one can gaze at them for a long time. In the same way, one never gets tired of some Butoh or Noh performances in which there is little movement.

Things moving slowly or not moving at all are not necessarily boring. For example in a zoo, the animals that move quickly such as monkeys or squirrels are not necessarily more amusing than animals who move less or more slowly such as crocodiles and elephants. Think about a snake; one may stare at the animal and its unpredictable movements in order not to miss the precise moment in which it moves.

A minimal movement is impressive if produced by something that is practically immobile.

However, banal dancers are boring even when doing rapid movements. The same goes for movies with predictable plots, even if they are action-packed. *In these cases, we can say that it is not the slowness which makes things boring.*

For some people, Noh and Japanese classical dance are boring, while others find contemporary music and arts boring. However, whether traditional or contemporary, things usually defined as boring are often those that one does not understand, know very well or know at all.

If one has some knowledge of Noh theater songs, the background of works and performers, one can appreciate a show. If one finds these performances boring, this is due to a lack of knowledge and not because of the artists.

Besides boredom, a feeling is also about the emotional intensity produced by the object observed. For example, in the Luxembourg Gardens in Paris we can often see couples sitting still, close together for more than half an hour; since the time they spend together is pleasant, they do not get bored even if nothing happens. However, if they sat for a long time with a person towards whom they had no feeling, it would be completely different. This principle also applies to the fact that we never get tired of watching our favorite actor for hours.

To conclude, here is a reproach to those who put on a boring show:

~ Information given to the audience is too sparse and of too poor quality in relation to the time spent at the show.

~ The quality of the performance is low.

~ The performance is predictable and leaves no room for surprise.

So, please do not be afraid that slow movements will bore the audience. The ultimate goal is a high-quality dance which is unpredictable and rich in information even if slow. If I got bored watching some performances, it was not only due to their slowness in development, but mainly because of their lack of content. Richness in content is the responsibility of choreographers and dancers.

~ 3.9 ~

Kosoku Mai

In this section I will talk about *Kosoku Mai* by introducing a series of exercises to be done blindfolded. This is a form of expression that I created in the mid-90s when I still lived in Tokyo.

The principle of *Kosoku Mai* is to impose a constraint on a part of the body to favor the function and movement of the other parts. Imposing a physical constraint on oneself entails challenging the human body and spirit in order to develop new skills and more freedom. It also allows you to transform yourself. The *Kosoku Mai* method has been covered quite a bit in the media and it is recognized as an integral part of the Alishina method.

Effectively representative of *Kosoku Mai*, *Blind Blink* was presented in Japan for the first time in 1995, then in Israel, Germany and France. In this dance I play a blind woman accompanied by a man who helps her to move (this role is played by a male dancer). This performance has experimental value:

Photo: Francis Lepage
Dancer: Juju Alishina,
1997 Paris

what are the limits of dance when one is blind? It is also a drama where the master and servant relationship is inverted. This recalls the relationship between the person who is blindfolded and the partner who protects them in Part 3, 3.7 *Strengthening the five senses*.

Blind Blink was presented in Paris in 1997 when I was invited to the first occasion of the *Festival de L'Imaginaire*, an international festival organized by the *Maison des Cultures du Monde*. This festival still takes place annually and includes artists from all over the world.

When *Blind Blink* was presented in Paris, the *Kosoku Mai* was described as follows:

> *"In the 80s the appearance of post-Butoh […] in which bodies are less exposed but the resolutely contemporary movement expresses a new rebellion."* It's this new aesthetic that we can link to Juju Alishina.

> Drawn from the series of *Kosoku Mai*, *Blind Blink* describes, through the portrait of a blind woman, the passion of the senses when a part of the body is subjugated or impeded. In a state of deliberate and artificial blindness, Juju Alishina is free from a certain "visual prohibition." A dancer, Kakuya Ohashi, helps her devotedly and breaks her world violently.

> […]

> For Juju Alishina, finding new interdisciplinary aesthetics is more important than conforming to predefined forms of avant-garde dance. In a permissive society where all expression is reduced to the same value, she questions the notion of avant-garde, which in her opinion limits Butoh to a bodily expression of the opposition between Eros and Thanatos.[1]

The idea of dancing limited by blindness came from my not having good eyesight. If I do not wear my contact lenses, the world appears to me like a Claude Monet painting. In the 80s and 90s, I lost my lenses so often on the stage and they were very expensive at that time. I stopped

---

1   Françoise Gründ

wearing them and I constantly had difficulty due to my poor eyesight. I wondered whether it would be possible to create a dance based on this limit of blindness by indicating this very clearly to the audience: this is the origin of *Kosoku Mai*.

Nowadays contact lenses have improved and so I now dance wearing them.

Exercises with the *Kosoku Mai*

We have already practiced exercises blindfolded (see Part 2, 2.4 and Part 3, 3.7 and 3.8). Below, I will introduce other *Kosoku Mai* improvisation exercises.

Limits imposed on the lower part of the body
Keeping one's heels up (individual/group)

All students should improvise using the whole space. The only restriction is that one cannot put one's heels on the floor, but all other movements are allowed. You can stand against a wall or pillar, sit or lie down as long as your heels do not touch the ground. Those who touch the ground with their heels must sit and become spectators waiting for the others to finish the exercise.

When I invented this exercise at the end of 2005 in Paris, all my students were able to keep their heels up for 30 minutes. Dancing for a long time without putting your heels on the ground is very hard, but if you combine upright and sitting positions, you should be able to do this for quite a long time.

During a session in 2008 I first asked all the students to do this exercise; I then split them into two groups so that they could observe each other. This is an interesting process to study.

The mermaid

The Rodin museum in the seventh arrondissement of Paris is located in a beautiful house with a large, well-kept garden. I had the opportunity to dance there during an event organized at the museum. One of my favorite sculptures by Rodin, *Les Sirènes* (the mermaids), is on display there.

- ↄ   Bind your legs with string to transform them into a mermaid tail (individual/group).

  - ↄ   Train with the tail while sitting with your legs stretched forward.

  - ↄ   Train by lying on your stomach with the tail towards the back.

  - ↄ   Train by lying on your side with the tail on the side.

  - ↄ   Move forwards, backwards, left, right; roll your body.

  The constraint affects only the lower part of the body: unlike a fish, as a human being you can use your torso.

  Students move around the space from one side to another, one by one in the mermaid position. Each student is required to find their own way to move. After this class, one student said: "It all became easier when I imagined that there was water all around and my body was floating."

- ↄ   Form pairs and find a way to communicate by keeping the mermaid position. Since one cannot interlace legs when the lower part of the body is bound, contact with other mermaid or merman students seems very sweet and innocent even when lying down.

- ↄ   Create some waving movements and a short dance in which mermaids arrive with the waves (group). The text below deals with the mermaid exercise and describes my method.

JUJU ALISHINA: THE EXPRESSIVE POWER OF THE BODY

A frail silhouette, long black hair, a charming smile and a shy beauty…despite her fragile appearance, almost evanescent, Juju Alishina, dancer and choreographer, captures gazes. Offstage, this Japanese woman born in Kobe is a wife and a mother like many others. On the stage, with her frozen features, she embodies an almost mystical feminine figure.

Today she chooses the *mermaid*. Clasped legs and crossed feet to imitate a fish tail, bodies perform, tangle up, and dance with one another in a sort of aquatic ballet. Some laughter bursts out here and there. Two by two, then all together, participants wave and contort, jostle and skim past each other, performing as they can, deprived of the use of their legs on the floor.

Improvisation, performing and the reflection of a natural element, an animal or a human being; the true essence of Juju's work lies in these elements. Her approach to Butoh is far from conventional: it is body training and an impressive emotional release at the same time; a mix of contemporary features and Japanese traditions.

"Juju invites us to find our own dance. She leads us down new paths to explore through our body and emotions. Then, we all have to make our own way through," says Catherine, one of her students.

In Juju's art, the body is shown dramatically, as in a kabuki performance. Each pose, with its pure lines, is charged with strong evocative power; love, death, fear, cruelty, etc., can be seen in each attitude; they are embodied by Juju, perfectly lit by the spotlights.

DANCER TO HER VERY FINGERTIPS

This exuberant imagination, this avidity for new experiences and this openness characterize the artistic personality of Juju Alishina.[2]

The *Byakko-sha* company also performed the mermaid dance with a costume formed by a tailfin-shaped sack which kept one's legs in place.

At a workshop in Germany in 1999 where I participated as a teacher, the English dancer Miriam King also taught how the legs should be crossed.

---

2   Françoise Diboussi, *BITO Web-magazine*, August 2006.

Limits imposed on the upper part of the body

To immobilize oneself, one can be tied with string, one's hands can be tied or handcuffs can be worn.

A piece of dance called *bo shibari* (tied to a stick) forms the basis of a *Kyogen theatre* play.[3] The climax of the performance is when the actors are dancing: the *Taro kaja*[4] dances with his hands tied behind his back and the other, the *Jiro kaja*,[5] dances with his hands tied to a stick so that he cannot drink sake.

I have often practiced the *Kosoku Mai* of the torso with a sword balanced on my head. One pivots or lifts up a leg keeping one's head immobile. This creates suspense and captures the audience's attention because nobody knows when the sword will fall. This technique comes from oriental dance. In order to immobilize my head, as well as the sword, I have often used a cup with a lighted candle as well.

In addition, one can consider the *suriashi* in Part 2, 2.5 as a form of *Kosoku Mai* since the upper part of the body does not move.

Improvisation with a plastic bottle

Place an empty plastic bottle on its side and hold it at each end. In this way you will improvise keeping your hands occupied, so that the mobility of your chest and back is greater than when you have your hands tied. You can therefore apply more force to a specific point. Generally when improvising, one tends to think about one's hands and arms. When your arms and hands are fixed in place, you can focus more attention on the other parts of the body. The result is better movement control. If you want to improve your muscle strength, do this exercise with a bottle full of water.

In the following exercise, dance holding an imaginary bottle. I often use this technique for my dances (see picture on page 273).

---

3   N.d.T.: *Kyogen*, literally "mad words" or "wild speech," is a form of traditional Japanese comic theater. It developed contemporarily with Noh, was performed along with Noh as an intermission of sorts between Noh acts, on the same stage, and retains close links to Noh in the modern day; therefore, it is sometimes designated *Noh-kyōgen*.

4   N.d.T.: *Taro kaja*: main servant, literally "(common name) + servant."

5   N.d.T: *Jiro kaja*: second servant, literally "second son + servant."

The method, consisting of removing the elements with which one has trained, gives more realistic power to your movements. For example, in the exercise in which two people play with an imaginary balloon (see Part 2, 2.4), there will be a considerable difference in the quality of movement if one trains with a real balloon first in order to feel and internalize the weight and sensation.

Although it is not possible to cover everything in only one book, this method includes numerous exercises utilizing plastic bottles. These exercises have been inspired by the use of dumbbells.

Training with dumbbells enhances muscle strength. However, their weight makes them difficult to transport, especially when flying. I thus started to use plastic bottles instead so I can train every day.

Plastic bottles of mineral water are cheap and they can be bought all over the world. Furthermore, by filling up a bottle the weight will always be the same (1.5 liters are equal to 1.5 kg—about 3.3 pounds). If one trains with different weights on the right and left hands there will be disequilibrium that will lead to harmful repercussions for the body. It is really important that the weight is spread equally. If one needs to add some weight, just calculate how many bottles are needed and put them in a bag.

Kosoku Mai and eroticism

I have already dealt with the *oiran* walk in Part 2, 2.5 and 2.8. This walk may be considered to be a sort of *Kosoku Mai.*

In his book *The Unfashionable Human Body*, Bernard Rudofsky wrote of *oiran* walking:

During the sixteenth and seventeenth centuries the wearing of stilted shoes became fashionable in other European countries [...] The continued attraction of the portable footstools was based on their instability; the sight of a woman walking precariously closely corresponded to man's image of feminine helplessness.

In the Far East, the Japanese *oiran* wore 30-cm-high *getas* (about 12 inches) which symbolized their occupation. In order to walk without losing her balance, an *oiran* must be supported by two assistants. Her gait is so slow that she seems almost pathetic. A critic said that the sight of an *oiran* dragging her heavy wooden *getas* on tiptoe is an extremely sensual scene; the practice which consists of impairing or exhibiting a part of the female body is thus less common today since it is considered a social taboo.

What is said above about the *oiran* walk can be applied to the *Kosoku Mai* as well.

According to Havelock Ellis in *Studies in the Psychology of Sex*: "Pain itself, [...] may, under a great variety of special circumstances, become an erotic symbol and afford the same relief as the emotions normally accompanying the sexual act."

Physical handicaps can increase sexual excitement or the visual effect, such as in Chinese foot-binding. When two participants (a man and a woman) do the exercise of guiding a blind person (Part 3, 3.7) sometimes this provokes a sort of sensual emotion. This is probably because one is supposed to abandon one's body to someone else's hands.

Dance of a pregnant woman: fiction and reality

When a pregnant dancer performs, this can be considered *Kosoku Mai* since she is forced to limit her movements. Of course, we do not practice the *Kosoku Mai* by actually becoming blind or truly cutting off our arms. The important thing is that *Kosoku Mai* is practiced to improve sensation and technique.

I did actually perform on stage when I was eight months pregnant. This performance was a true *Kosoku Mai* and not fictional. This was a performance that I could do only once in my life. It was even mentioned in the book *Butô(s)*.

I would not try to find a pregnant dancer to do this choreography again; when I recall it, I realize that it was incredibly dangerous. If you are a woman, please take care of your body, stop dancing during pregnancy and start dancing again only after having recovered little by little. This is the best way to keep on dancing and take care of one's health.

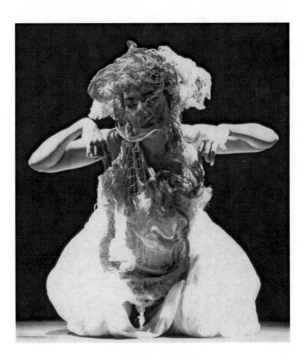

Photo: Francis Lepage
Dancer: Juju Alishina
Paris 1998

After this show, spectators were astonished and everyone asked if I was really pregnant. The power of authenticity always impresses the audience.

However, this can become a dangerous notion. Some choreographers use real blind, deaf-dumb or handicapped people to perform on stage. I think that this kind of show can be impressive, but according to this way of thinking, dancers should truly shed their blood, get injured or have sex on stage to stun the audience.

Obviously, there is a difference between a blind person dancing and a dancer playing the role of a blind person. What I aim at is to remain committed throughout the fiction on stage.

The issue of fiction and reality has long been discussed by those interested in performing art. One can grasp the complexity of this issue, for example when an actor truly sheds tears on stage; this act can be appreciated or considered contemptible since it can be regarded as unorthodox.

When beginners or young people take to the stage, they must look for reality. However, *professionals should look for techniques allowing them to create a "fiction which can prevail over reality."*

~ 3.10 ~

Creation and evaluation

To conclude a workshop which is open to all levels, I suggest the following exercises.

Group creation

Forming groups

Groups are composed of five or six people. The teacher can form groups of people who are at the same level or can form them randomly.

Organizing a performance

For example:

~ *Date:* the last day of the workshop.

~ *Place:* the training space used for the workshop (each group will decide on the setting and the number of chairs for the audience).

~ *Performance time:* 15 minutes.

~ *Music:* no music, just the sound produced by dancers through movements or voices.

~ *Costume:* training kit (no costumes needed).

~ *Rehearsal duration:* three to four hours.

~ *Audience:* workshop participants (sometimes friends or relatives are invited).

Other rules:

~ It is best not to have a leader. All members of the group make decisions together about the choreography and the staging.

~ The dance must be based on the techniques and movements learned during the workshop.

~ The group chooses a title.

Deciding on a topic

Sometimes participants work on a topic chosen by the teacher; here instead, we are going to see how the teacher leads the students through the choice of a topic.

The day before the topic is chosen, the teacher will make students play a word association game and will ask them to choose one of the words mentioned during the game.

Development

The teacher tells one of the participants a word. This person then says the first word that comes to mind. Several words are therefore collected (the goal is not to produce a semantic field; one must only consider the previous word, not the entire series of terms proposed. The result will be a group of words not necessarily connected to one another).

Such words could include:

~ Japan

~ Sun

~ Sea bathing

~ Jellyfish

~ Poison

~ Pain

~ Love

~ Happiness

~ Family

~ Canada

~ Franklin (a Canadian cartoon)

~ Ours (Franklin best friend)

~ Hunting rifle

~ Trial

~ Jail

~ Letter

~ Lovers

~ Darkness

~ Candle.

I enjoy playing this game. It allows the teacher and students to learn something new about other cultures. This game takes a lot of time. You should play it on the penultimate day.

The teacher gives all the words gathered to each group. Taking inspiration from these words, students create a dance.

Sometimes the teacher gives students a topic and asks them to create choreography connected to it. Up to now I have given topics made up of simple words like "key," "door," "travel" or "labyrinth" which can easily stimulate the imagination.

Rehearsal

The teacher gives a location to each group to create a dance and rehearse. Then the teacher observes each group by going between them. Sometimes I agree to split a group in two if people really disagree but this rarely happens.

Suggestions

If participants want to keep their performance a secret so that it will be a surprise, I do not intervene in the various stages of creation. Usually I give advice to each group.

Performing

Spectators sit in a designated area. The group giving the performance announces the title. The teacher watches the time (15 minutes). The teacher indicates to the students when to start and finish and tells them when five minutes are left, and then when one minute is left before the end.

Discussion and evaluation

Once the performances have finished, a discussion can take place. Students often say that the classes they attended, which seemed at the beginning to be unrelated, created a connection in their body. From a pedagogical standpoint, this creative stage at the end of the workshop is very useful for the students to arrive at this synthesis by themselves. Thanks to this last stage, the teacher can also check the results of his or her teaching.

Regarding classes organized at a school, I ask students to write a final report a week after the last class. Then I give them marks. I do not evaluate the participants in a workshop, but if they ask for individual guidance, I try to be as precise as possible.

Evaluation

Whether talking about dance, sport or science, people who daily strive to improve and develop their abilities often want to be evaluated for the work they have done. How should one deal with this in dance?

Whether a dancer passes an audition does not depend on the quality of dance produced. The aim of an audition is to select people for a certain performance or work, not to evaluate the dancer.

As far as I know, unlike ballet dancers, Butoh dancers have never been evaluated. Competitions are also unsuitable for expressing appreciation for Butoh dancers, because this appreciation is incompatible with preestablished criteria. Even if a Butoh dancer's skills can be easily identified through his or her career or the results obtained, evaluating his or her qualities seems difficult; this might be due to the fact that Butoh seems to defy all criteria and evaluation.

Evaluation at a school

In a school, students must somehow be evaluated, since their admission to a higher level or gaining a diploma depends on their results. Evaluation must therefore be meticulous and reliable.

Evaluation must involve certain criteria. Without criteria evaluation would be impossible. As I have already mentioned, there are no real criteria for Butoh evaluation; however, these do exist for dance in general. When I was teaching at Denison University in the United States as assistant professor, I evaluated the students according to the criteria below that I established by referring to the evaluation charts of the other professors.

EVALUATION	
Attendance, participation	20%
Attitude and progress	20%
Midterm exams: written test + dance test (topic given by the professor)	30%
Final exam: dance test (topic given by the professor + creation) + report	30%

The evaluation system of American universities is as follows (getting an F means repeating a class).

A=93–100; A–=90–92; B+=87–89; B=83–86; B–=80–82; C+=77–79; C=73–76; C–=70–72; D+=67–69; D=63–66; D–=60–62; F=<60.

"Attendance" and "attitude and progress" are of great importance, i.e. 40 percent of the total. This comes from the American principle that all efforts should be rewarded with a good grade.

In the solo dance test, students work on a topic given by the professor and they are evaluated according to the marks gained for their musicality, form and overall quality. For the creation test, composition and expression skills will be integrated into the evaluation criteria. When performing a duo, harmony with one's partner will also be considered.

Teamwork

When you dance with others, your goal must be to improve the overall quality of the dance. If you focus your attention on all the parts of the dance and not only yours, you will improve your own dance as a result.

The best method is to give a "role" to each dancer. One must decide who will be the main dancer; however, those playing a secondary role must also do their best. It is very important that each person knows their position on stage for each phase of the performance.

There is no point breaking the overall balance with competition or complaining about being in the background. For the performance to be brilliant, dancers must help each other.

When dancers develop good relationships and harmony, this greatly enhances the quality of the performance and conveys their joy to the audience.

The chart above is just an example; sometimes evaluation is more approximate. Some professors evaluate just by considering attendance and by providing a one-page report at the end of the semester. However, students prefer to be evaluated with a detailed chart that can constitute the starting point for improving their dance. The important thing is not the grade itself, but an awareness of one's level in order to progress.

Professor Gill Miller, doctor of anatomy, used to comment on her students' grades in great detail. When I had the opportunity to read her comments and I thought about the time she had spent on this, I nearly fainted. How lucky her students must be to have a professor like this! Students are often dissatisfied with their grades: this way of grading should convince them.

Evaluation outside of schools in contests

Out of school, some commercial factors should be added to the evaluation criteria. For example, fine art contests attract the interest of many people; this factor helps enrich this market: thanks to contests, new talents can be discovered; organizers, jury members and the prize winners all have a purpose.

When talking about a school, economics are usually not considered. Even if one has gained excellent results, one might not earn one's living from dance. Why not create a dance contest based not only on artistic and pedagogical values, but also on commercial perspectives? This would represent an important event in the artistic field and would help future dancers start their professional careers.

Evaluation of choreographers

This kind of evaluation depends on the management of the choreographer's company. Finance, turnover and social contributions do not directly pertain to dance. However, the evaluation of a company is certainly connected to the evaluation of the choreographer, so the choreographer cannot neglect the management of the company and the creation of dances.

The number of prizes won in contests is another criterion which should be considered when evaluating a choreographer.

Choreography competitions

Nowadays, there are many choreography competitions and an eagerness to award prizes. I have been on the jury for a French competition for young choreographers. In my opinion, such competitions are not always impartial, since the circumstances in which a choreographer creates largely differ. If I organized a competition I would ask candidates to create a work of ten or 20 minutes in two hours' time under the same conditions (budget, team, place, materials and so forth). The theme and conditions would be announced on-site. They would then depend only on their knowledge, technique, judgment and management skills—on their creativity. Their true skills would thus be challenged.

In the United States, there is a television cookery show called *Iron Chef America* which is broadcast by the Food Network and is inspired by a Japanese program called *Ryôri No Tetsujin* broadcast by Fuji Television. It seems that it has obtained the highest viewing figures for the channel. I very much enjoyed watching it when I was in the United States.

One of the three celebrity chefs and a challenger must compete based on a theme, which is announced on the spot, using the tools, assistants and products provided by a certain deadline. I really loved this program for its spectacular features: the set and screenplay are outstanding, there is a lot of suspense and there is above all an authentic attitude among the chefs towards their job. If a similar program were ever created for choreography, I really would like to direct it.

Let's return to the workshop. The last day of the workshop and at the end of the second semester of school I usually organize a party. This takes place in the training space, at a restaurant or a café. Sometimes I invite students to my home as well. This provides an occasion for the participants to recover from their efforts made during exercises and discuss and exchange ideas. It also represents the grand finale of our time spent together.

AFTERWORD

The core of the Alishina method is to show, very clearly and concretely, the means for reaching a higher artistic level. The targets are: to provide basic tools to form one's body; to explore the opportunities provided by dance, staging and improvisation while considering different perspectives; to increase endurance; and to optimize the quality of performance.

Now that you know the Alishina method, let's review what you have learned.

~ Knowing your body's capabilities in order to adapt your body and develop its functions.

~ Learning how to use Qi.

~ Learning to collaborate and be in harmony with others.

~ Developing the imagination and refining the five senses to enrich the expression of the body.

~ Learning kata movements and studying their developmental process.

~ Discovering beauty and new concepts.

~ Acquiring the ability to manipulate and handle time and space on stage.

Content of expression

You will have noticed that this book deals with *expression techniques* but does not deal extensively with *content*. This is because content cannot be learned at school or through a book; it can only be acquired throughout a lifetime.

I believe in training my students with honesty and love, but I abstain from any intrusion into their private lives. Some methods are similar to psychosocial techniques whose goal is to define the psychic trauma of each student to find the most suitable content for each one. I believe that perseverance and constant body training will lead to mental healing as well, and that *entering into the mysteries of the technique will lead to improvements in mental health.*

Sometimes a new idea prevails over previous research; sometimes what was in vogue ten years ago goes out of fashion. The spirit of content is flighty and uncertain. However, a well-trained body and good technique will never betray us. You will be rewarded according to the efforts you make. Success will surely come if you stay humble and keep working hard.

Even if you are able to use your body to express content or ideas which are not yours, you will never perform satisfactorily if you do not feel any empathy. This is why this book is based on technique. Moreover, I think that those attending my classes or using this book all have something to express.

At my classes, I often meet people who already have some concepts and come to class to improve their technique; the opposite—enough technique but no concept—rarely occurs.

I developed the desire to follow a technique when I needed to get back on the right track and I was lost in a sort of dark labyrinth, unable to progress. The forms of theater and dance that I practiced at that time (in my teens) were too idealistic and abstract.

In a book called *20-Seiki no Buyoh* (*Dance in the 20th Century*), Kazuo Kamizawa (1929–2003) stresses that the Butoh method by Tatsumi Hijikata often lacks basic training related to ways of using the body. I suppose that he did not have the time to systematize all these exercises. But he then adds: someday someone will be able to meet this need.

The Butoh school to which I belonged also lacked a certain logic and coherence. Nevertheless I turned that weakness into strength, as people naturally tend to try to make up for what they lack. I was therefore compelled to build a basic technique starting from my own experience.

What I learned from life in the group at *Byakko-sha* does not only rely on dance technique but on the following:

~ The basic thought that life itself is Butoh

~ We do our best even when accomplishing a small task

~ Never abandon the stage.

The experiences I had there could only have occurred in that "last underground age." They are therefore precious to me and always remain very special. Only today do I realize that they have become the core of my dance content: they influenced me more in content than technique.

Note for teachers

My point of view on teaching is to convey to students all that I know. This does not necessarily mean that students will lose their originality. On the contrary, sharing with others is truly enriching. Teachers do not need to be afraid of losing their knowledge. Since I currently give regular classes, I can carry out my ideas in one week's time, which is very helpful.

When you free your mind, space is made for new ideas and improvements gradually develop. If your mind is too full of incubating ideas, of course they can develop, but what often happens is that you get tired or just forget them.

If you are not committed to training, education or research for future generations and you are satisfied just with performing, technique and method stagnate and the human relationship turns into business. The number of spectators and performance profits might become the most fundamental features.

The only categories of people who can truly offer reprimand beyond any self-interest or egotism are parents and teachers, since their unique goal is the well-being of those whom they are addressing. *In education, there is a real human contact which goes beyond business*: teaching is driven by the desire to educate with care, tenderness and much selflessness. If you do not commit to transmitting your knowledge, your art will disappear with you. What one can learn from the teacher is not only a dance technique. Education concerns the global human development of an individual.

Note for students

In this book we have dealt with a number of training exercises and dances. Now, I would ask you: what is most important to you? The answer is to continue dancing and never lose your passion. Perseverance is essential. Do not give up after having made little effort.

Developing dance skills depends on the person: some progress gradually; others progress suddenly after a long period of stagnation. There are people who stagnate after rapid progress and who then start to progress visibly when they start thinking that they have reached their limit. If you keep training long enough, you will realize this yourself. If you leave as soon as you encounter difficulty, you will never progress.

Some very agile people are satisfied with practicing little technique and think that since one thing is easy, they can move on to the next. Moving on to another thing before working thoroughly on a technique can lead only to superficial outcomes, no matter the field.

If someone clumsy has spent ten years doing something that another person can do in a day, these ten years have not been spent in vain since they were full of thought and reflection. Thanks to this timelapse, the person will not only have acquired the technique but all the other techniques connected to it as well. A technique acquired after ten years of work is like fine wine.

Enhancing one's technique always involves mental and human development.

There is no know-how which enables one to attain absolute success in dance or art in general. Depending on the timing and environment, know-how will also change. In the same way, in the performing arts, the concept of success depends on the point of view and objectives of each individual. At least one can create a method which helps everyone to be successful.

Note for professional dancers

My role is training new talent. When I think about their future careers, I realize that it is essential for them to have a system (e.g. employment) and environment in which to dance. Creating these systems and environments involves a great deal of work that cannot be done quickly or only through my own resources. Change requires the awareness of all those interested in dance.

Becoming and remaining a professional dancer or choreographer is not easy. We must lead a life whose rhythm is the opposite to that of ordinary people; for example, we must work when others are resting or having fun. I have often been seriously injured and have shed blood, sweat and tears more than once. Even if I work every day from morning to night, I often wonder about my future resources. I could not attend my mother's funeral, the weddings of my family members or my son's school ceremonies. I have consecrated my body and soul to dance, leaving my private life behind.

However, I realized that dance allowed me to have a lot of different experiences. I traveled the world and I was granted access to places that most people never see. I have met a lot of people. Thanks to dance I also met my husband and moved to France.

Being a professional dancer and choreographer is not always rosy but I confess that looking back on life, I have no regrets.

My wishes for the future

This book was published in Japan in 2010 by Shinsui Sha. When it was published I returned to Tokyo for the first time after 13 years in France. A conference, a book-signing and a Butoh workshop were held to promote my book. It was praised by the Japanese press and I had favorable reviews from dance teachers and dance school directors.

People living in Japan could not see my performances nor participate in my classes. This book allows them to do exercises and share in my teaching method even at a distance. In 2013, the French version of this book was published by Éditions L'Harmattan. Most of my students have bought the book and refer to it both before and after lessons. Some people came to Paris after reading the book to experience the method directly with their own bodies.

I hope that my method keeps evolving, spreads all over the world and is conveyed to future generations as Pilates and Laban were. Following a method not only involves doing the exercises that it contains, but also agreeing with and sharing the underlying ideas and aesthetics.

The human body is of great value. I believe that in *future society, the only thing that will still have value will be direct experience.* With the development of the internet and information technology, the acquisition of knowledge without true experience has become a common currency.

Challenge!
Learn!
Confront your own karma!
Fight!
Surpass yourself!
Never give up your passion for art!

Through this book, I hope from the bottom of my heart to contribute to the creation of a suitable environment for the development of dance for future generations.

Finally, I would like to thank all the people who have contributed to the publication of this book in English. Special thanks go to Jessica Kingsley Publishers, the translator, Corinna Torregiani, the proofreader, Jessica Weiss, and Michiko Suzuki who translated the text from Japanese into French; thanks too to the photographers and all those who helped me in fulfilling this project.

Juju Alishina
Paris, July 2015

BIBLIOGRAPHY

Benjamin, W. and Arendt, H. (eds) (1968) *The Work of Art in the Age of Mechanical Reproduction, Illuminations*. London: Fontana.

Diboussi, F. (2006) "Juju Alishina: le pouvoir expressif du corps." (JuJu Alishina: the expressive power of the body) *BITO Web-magazine*.

Grűnd, F. (1997) "Danse post—Butô." (Post Butoh dance) *Catalogue du Premier festival de l'Imaginaire*. Paris: MCM.

Hanayagi, C. (2008) *Fundamentals of Japanese Dance (Kabuki Dance)*. Trans. Leonard Pronko and Takao Tomono. Tokyo: Kodansha Shuppan Service Center Ltd.

Hare, T. B. (1996) *Zeami's Style: the Noh Plays of Zeami Motokiyo*. Stanford, CA: Stanford University Press.

Hare, T. B. (2008) *Zeami, Performance Notes*. New York: Columbia University Press.

Havelock, E. (2013) *Studies in the Psychology of Sex. Project Gutenberg*. Available at www.gutenberg.org/ebooks/13614, accessed on 5 June 2015.

Hearn, L. (1984) *Glimpses of Unfamiliar Japan*. Volume 2. Boston, MA: Houghton, Mifflin and Company.

Holborn, M. and Hoffman, E. (1987) *Butoh. Dance of the Dark Soul*. New York: Aperture.

Horton, F. S. (1999) *Dancing into Darkness: Butoh, Zen and Japan*. Pittsburgh, PA: University of Pittsburgh Press.

Kamizawa, K. (1990) *20 seiki no buyô*. Tokyo: Mirai-sha.

Keene, D. (2010) *So Lovely a Country Will Never Perish: Wartime Diaries of Japanese Writers*. New York: Columbia University Press.

Kerber, K. L. (2005) *Erotic Symbolism*. New Delhi: Global Vision Publishing House.

Mitchell, J. D. (1994) *Staging Japanese Theatre: Noh and Kabuki: Ikkaku sennin (The Holy Hermit Unicorn) and Narukami (The Thunder God)*. Key West, FL: Institute for Advanced Studies in the Theatre Arts Press in association with Florida Keys Educational Foundation, Florida Keys Community College.

Nagai, K. (1967) "Odoriko." *Nihon Bungaku Zenshu 11*, Nagai Kafû Shû. Tokyo: Kawade Shobo Shinsa.

Novack, C. J. (1990) *Sharing the dance. Contact Improvisation and American Culture.* Madison, WI: The University of Wisconsin Press.

Ortolani, B. (1995) *The Japanese Theatre: From Shamanistic Ritual to Contemporary Pluralism.* Revised edition. Princeton, NJ: Princeton University Press.

Pace, A. (2007) End-of-semester Report at Denison University.

Rossi, A. W. (2001) "Fashion and foot deformation. The need for podiatrists to deal with human nature." *Podiatry Management October,* 103–118.

Rudofsky, B. (1971) *The Unfashionable Human Body.* Garden City, NY: Doubleday and Company, Inc.

Tarliel, J. (2003) "BUTO—Exteriorisez-vous." (Butoh—externalize!) *Votre Beauté* October. Available at www.votrebeaute.fr, accessed on 15 May 2015.

Wilson, W. S. (2006) *The Flowering Spirit: Classic Teachings on the Art of Nō.* Tokyo: Kodansha International, Yamazaki.

Zeami, M. (1975) *Fûshikaden, or, The Fûshikaden. (Style and the Flower)* Trans. Shohei Shimada, Nara: n.p.

BIOGRAPHY

JUJU ALISHINA
Japanese dancer and choreographer

Juju Alishina
Photo: Jean-Claude Flaccomio 2009

Born in Kobe in 1963, Juju Alishina trained as a traditional Japanese dancer and has worked in Butoh since 1982. In 1990 in Tokyo, she founded her own dance company, Nuba, in the pursuit of a new style of Butoh.

Having assimilated many different styles and approaches to dance, she has developed her own unique and original movements, exploiting the possibilities of eastern dance to their fullest.

She is considered an important figure in the third generation of Butoh, as she has created a "fine blend of traditional and avant-garde" styles.

The trademark of the Nuba dance company is its paradoxical combination of shadow and celebration. While remaining loyal to the ceremonies of ancient Japan and eastern dance in general, it is an exciting new approach to Butoh.

In 1998, Juju Alishina moved her company to Paris and since then has developed her own methods, both in Paris and abroad. Juju Alishina has also taught Japanese dance (traditional and Butoh) in universities in the USA.

Juju Alishina is often chosen as a representative of Japanese dance at important events in France and is a jury member in dance competitions. Since 2011, Juju Alishina has hosted improvisation sessions in Butoh known as "SOKKYO."

This book was first published in Japan in 2010 and the French translation followed in February 2013.

Juju Alishina regularly writes about various subjects for Japanese magazines. All the pictures in this book have been drawn by Juju Alishina.

Website: www.dansenuba.fr